teaching writers *to*

REFLECT

teaching writers *to*
REFLECT

Strategies for a More Thoughtful Writing Workshop

Anne Elrod Whitney

Colleen McCracken

Deana Washell

Heinemann

Portsmouth, NH

Heinemann

361 Hanover Street

Portsmouth, NH 03801–3912

www.heinemann.com

Offices and agents throughout the world

Library of Congress Cataloging-in-Publication Data

Names: Whitney, Anne Elrod, author. | McCracken, Colleen M., author. | Washell, Deana, author.

Title: Teaching writers to reflect : strategies for a more thoughtful writing workshop / Anne Elrod Whitney, Colleen McCracken, Deana Washell.

Description: Portsmouth, NH : Heinemann, [2019] | Includes bibliographical references.

Identifiers: LCCN 2018047235 | ISBN 9780325076867

Subjects: LCSH: English language—Composition and exercises—Study and teaching (Elementary). | Language arts (Elementary). | Reflective learning. | Mindfulness (Psychology).

Classification: LCC LB1576 .W486288 2019 | DDC 372.6—dc23

LC record available at https://lccn.loc.gov/2018047235

Editor: Katie Wood Ray

Production editor: Sonja S. Chapman

Interior and cover designs: Vita Lane

Cover image: © Mindstyle/Getty Images

Author photograph: Katie Brumberg Photography, LLC

Typesetter: Valerie Levy, Drawing Board Studios

Manufacturing: Val Cooper

Printed in the United States of America on acid-free paper

23 22 21 20 19 RWP 1 2 3 4 5

For the young writers who give us so much to think and talk about.
Everything in this book we have learned from you.

CONTENTS

ONE Why Reflection?

TWO Writers Remember

THREE   Writers Describe   45

FOUR   Writers Act   67

FIVE From Reflection to Self-Assessment   91

Acknowledgments

Our three names are on the front of this book, but the work described inside would not be possible without the help of a brave and supportive community.

It was Jill Corkery who first suggested that Colleen and Deana consider teaming up, who later suggested to Anne that she should check out their writers' workshop, and who nudged and reminded until we all finally got together. We're grateful to Jill and all of the instructional coaches in the State College Area School District for inspiring and encouraging a culture of professional learning.

Mike Maclay and Danielle Yoder, the former and current principals of Easterly Parkway Elementary School, took both symbolic and practical steps to make this work possible, carving out time and resources for our collaboration. Superintendent Robert O'Donnell and Assistant Superintendent of Elementary Education Vernon Bock, along with the school board of the State College Area School District, supported us by approving Anne's presence in the district as a researcher and honoring Deana and Colleen's commitment to professional growth.

Day to day at Easterly Parkway Elementary, too many saints to name have stepped in and out of our writers' workshop with ideas, questions, and support: teachers, interns, supervisors, paraprofessionals, learning support and ESL providers all trusted us and learned with us.

The Department of Curriculum and Instruction at Penn State supported this work with a Research Initiation Grant, and Penn State graduate students Frances Bose and Yamil Sarraga-Lopez were especially helpful along the way.

We're still not quite over our shock at the privilege of working with *the* Katie Wood Ray as editor of this book. Working with her has been, we imagine, like being young writers in her class: we have had choice, inspiration, and time to experiment, all backed by such solid advice and such insightful and specific feedback from a writer who's been there, that we had no choice but to learn and improve. All of the good ideas here were profoundly shaped by Katie, and any bad ones are ours alone.

Most of all, we are grateful to the families who not only share their young writers with us every day, but also allowed us to study and write about their children. We hope our love for each writer and our belief in each one's potential is visible on every page of this book.

Foreword

Years ago I was conferring with a first grader named Lucas. It was January, and he was making a nonfiction book about eagles. He was illustrating a page where he'd written, "Eagles have sensitive eyes," and as we talked about how he knew this interesting fact, he asked me, "Do you know what I want to be when I grow up?"

"What?" I asked.

"A firefighter and an illustrator," he said.

"Really?"

He explained. "Yes, because it's a helpful job, and if I'm at home working on a book, I can just quit on it, and go to the fire, and when I get back home my book will still be there waiting on me. You can use all the time you want."

He knew this to be true, as he'd been working on his eagles book for many days and still had lots he wanted to do.

I've never forgotten this exchange. Of course the fact that I caught it on tape allows me to revisit it whenever I want, where I see a much younger version of both myself and the little boy with the wide smile and fabulous mullet ("All business in the front, all party in the back," he once told me) who's all grown up now.

And no, in case you're wondering, I don't know if his life plan worked out that way or not. But it was a good plan, wasn't it? I like helpful jobs. And illustrators.

What struck me that morning, and strikes me still, is how Lucas *knew* himself in that way. At the ripe old age of six, he'd had enough experience making books to understand the temporal nature of work that unfolds over time. He'd had enough experience to know that he was just the kind of person who could stay with a project, direct his own actions, and realize his intentions. He felt comfortable and confident enough in his work to imagine a future that included him doing it every day. It's what he wanted *to be*.

Well, actually, it was one of the things he wanted to be.

But think about how much puzzling through it must have taken for Lucas to figure out how he could manage his two dream jobs at the same time. Clearly, this young writer and illustrator was not just going through the motions; he was deeply reflective about his work.

I'm not at all surprised that I thought of Lucas when it came time to introduce you to *Teaching Writers to Reflect*. In so many ways, he represents precisely the vision Anne, Colleen, and Deana say they have for their students: "that their writing experiences be layered with rich reflection, so that as they write, they not only produce specific products, but they develop as writers who know *for themselves* what they are doing and why." In their classrooms, they pursue this vision with a laser sharp focus on the role that reflection plays in the construction of identity. They know that if children are to become agentive writers who can wield power with a pen or a keyboard, reflection will be key to that becoming.

Some children, no doubt, are just naturally reflective. I don't doubt that much of Lucas' thoughtfulness about his work was just part of who he is. But all children—and adults for that matter—can be taught to be more reflective. This teaching begins with building in time and expectation for reflection. It begins with simple questions: *What kind of writing do you most like to do? What's challenging for you about writing?* It begins with modeling, with children watching adults who stop in the middle of things to wonder aloud about something that's occurred.

What I learned from working with Anne, Colleen, and Deana on this book (I was privileged to be their editor), however, is that there is so much more we can do to teach children how to reflect, but we have to take this work on with intention. We can't leave it to chance. The frame they use for this teaching—remember, describe, act—is very intentional, it positions reflection at the center of writing workshop, and it represents a powerful habit of mind that can serve children across the day and throughout their lives, not just when they are writing.

I have been teaching in, researching through, and writing about workshops for many, many years now, and I truly believe that this piece of the work, the reflection piece, is what's missing in so many classrooms. And it's not missing because of anyone's willfulness or deliberate rejection of it. We're just busy. It's tough to get everything in as it is, so going through the motions helps us get wherever it is we're trying to go.

But in the lovely, authentic voices of Colleen's and Deana's second and third graders, I was reminded again and again throughout the book of how enormously valuable it is for children to stop, reflect, and think about who they are at one precious moment in time. Like their student Jim who said, "I wrote a book called "Sharks" and really like to write comic books, but I worry about Swiss cheese, spiders, and holes." When I read this I thought, "You know, Jim doesn't get this moment back. He will only be this writer with these joys and these worries once in his life. How lucky he is to have teachers who gave him time to stop and think about who he is in this moment."

Reflection gives us that. It gives us the chance to, as Lucy Calkins has said, hold our lives in our hands and declare them treasures. But it does so much more, of course (not that there needs to be anything more), and in this book the authors show us how students become *better writers* when they learn how to learn from their own experiences. Anne, Colleen, and Deana also show us how they become better teachers when they stop long enough to listen and learn from their students.

I love this little gem of a book. I believe it's got important work to do in the world. I love the fireflies on the cover. I know that if you are holding this book in your hands, you've caught the light of it and you can use it to brighten your path forward in this work.

No need to hurry.

As a little sage once taught me, you can use all the time you want.

—Katie Wood Ray

Introduction

REFLECTIVE STUDENTS, REFLECTIVE TEACHERS

This is a book about reflection in the context of teaching writing. We start with ourselves: we notice that our own teaching is richest when we find moments to step back and reflect—to think, talk, and write about what is going on in our classrooms and what we make of that going forward. We've found that the more we invest in reflection, the more we grow.

We think the same is true for kids. What if students were thinking about their work as writers as deeply as we think about our work as teachers? What if they not only wrote but could describe in detail what they were doing and why? What if each time they sat to write, they had at hand all of the things they'd tried and learned from so far? What if they knew themselves so well as writers that they had good intuition about what might and might not work for them when they ran into trouble in their writing?

This is our vision for our students: that their writing experiences be layered with rich reflection, so that as they write, they not only produce specific products but also develop as writers who know *for themselves* what they are doing and why. To accomplish this vision, we have to teach kids directly *how* to reflect on writing.

In this book, we invite you into our classroom, where we make vibrant, reflective writing and talking a daily part of how we work on writing. We invite you to follow us as we share how we teach students to reflect. We don't pretend that our teaching situation and your teaching situation are alike: if you've met one teacher, you've met one teacher, and we all have different contexts, different working conditions, and different resources and constraints shaping what we do. We can't promise easy answers or perfect success, but we can promise this: we will be authentic, showing you our real practices and real kids in pursuit of real learning. Before we get started, you should know a little of the story of how we came to center active, conscious reflection in our teaching.

Our reflection story began with our professional friendship. We (Deana and Colleen) were teachers in the same building who had gotten to know each other through the years as we worked together on curriculum committees, mentored student teaching interns, and developed science teacher education projects. As teacher colleagues, we grew to respect one another and the learning we could do together. Teaching writing was overwhelming, and sometimes hard to navigate, and we wanted help figuring things out day to day. "This job is too hard to do alone," we thought.

Around this time, the school district had also adopted a new resource for writing instruction. We began to meet to plan together and support one another as we used the new resource. At some point, we began to combine our classes for writing when it worked logistically to do so, and the following year we were even able to tweak our specials schedule to get twenty minutes or so of planning time in common twice a week. Later on, Anne, who had been working with district teachers leading professional development in writing, began to join us in these meetings and in the classroom.

In the first two or three years of our shared work around writing, reflection was not a focus. We each just wanted to have a thinking partner for the difficult work of teaching writing. But somewhere along our journey, there was a shift. The more we asked students to reflect, the more we did so ourselves. Modeling a reflective strategy at the board for our writers, it was impossible not to recall the same strategy twenty minutes later when we met to plan for the coming week. Often, we simply tried for ourselves the same strategies we had asked kids to use. Other times, our reflection was less structured but no less deliberate. As reflection became our habit, our thinking shifted from completing the "assignment" of planning together to reflecting more deeply and broadly about why we were doing things and how our actions impacted kids.

Through reflection, we and our students both have moved into a more purposeful, powerful role in the classroom. The students moved through reflection from "What do you [the teacher] want me to do with this text?" to "What can *I* do with this text?" Right alongside them, we teachers also became more comfortable going off book as we learned through students' reflections; for example, we discovered that Joaquin was a writer who was incredibly worried about spelling, so he produced little on paper until he was comfortable with taking a risk, and that Marcos was a writer who had an amazing voice that was rich in vocabulary but struggled to get ideas down coherently on paper. The more we learned about our students, the more we tailored our instruction to meet their own unique needs. This freed us to let go of asking, "What does the unit book say to do next?" and pushed us instead toward wondering, "What do *these writers* need right now, and what resources (including the unit book) can help us meet those needs?"

That's our story about the difference reflection has made for us as teachers. What might your story be? In the chapters that follow, we show you how we teach kids to reflect on what they do as writers using a three-step process: *remember, describe,* and *act.* We share specific teaching strategies we use for each component of the process, and we dramatize classroom scenes, narrate lessons, and show you our students' work so that you can see how to do the same with your own students. And along the way, we also offer invitations to *you* to reflect as a teacher, so you can experience the power of reflection for yourself.

chapter

ONE

Why Reflection?

On the next-to-last day of school, our second- and third-grade writers sat in a large circle, reflecting on the past year.

"I became better at coming up with ideas," said a writer who began the year sharpening his pencil, rolling on the carpet, or visiting the bathroom anytime we started to write—anything other than face his blank page.

"I have gotten better at writing for a longer time," said a writer who used to be that kid who ran up to the teacher after five minutes, claiming, "I'm done! Is this good?"

"I used to say, 'I can't do it!' and now I say, 'I can and I am doing it!'" reported a writer who, learning English, used to wait for a teacher's help before beginning anything.

"I think I got better at writing stories and drafts that I like, that when I read over it, I enjoyed it," explained a writer who, the year before, started piece after piece and then crumpled each one into the trash, claiming none of her starts was worth pursuing.

"I used to doubt myself a lot and worry about 'No, these ideas aren't good enough.' Now I trust my ideas a little more, so I can get more done. I can always go back later, but now I can write *something*," said a writer who used to agonize over every word before painstakingly writing anything down.

We're glad these kids felt like they'd accomplished something as writers, and we attest that they were right; they had come a long way in each of the areas they named. But even more, we're glad they *knew* enough about themselves as writers to make these comments. After a year of writing and reflecting on what they were doing as writers, they not only could say things about writing itself—about the genres they wrote in, about conventions—but also could talk about their own abilities and challenges and the processes by which they solved writing problems. They could do this because they knew how to reflect on what they did as writers.

Making the Case for Reflection

When student writers know how to reflect, they know how to learn from their writing experiences. Reflection has been called what "turn[s] experience into learning" (Boud, Keogh, and Walker 1985). It's one thing to experience something, but if the experience is then forgotten or not connected in any direct way to other experiences, how is it useful? Reflection is thinking about what has happened, making connections among parts of an experience, and naming aspects of it. Reflection is about processing an experience, noticing the feelings and memories it arouses, and linking it up to other kinds of experiences that relate to it (Dewey 1933). Through reflection, experiences are available to think about and learn from going forward, doing more of the same or doing differently as the situation demands. Reflection transforms a student's actions in the classroom from the empty satisfying of a teacher's assignments to a real learning experience that not only satisfies the teacher but also builds something lasting for the writer.

We teach reflection because of what it does for students, but it also helps *us* as teachers to better know what our students need. When students reflect on writing, they verbalize what they do and do not understand, what they struggle with, and what they did and thought as they worked through a writing problem. This helps us get inside their thinking. Writing is one of those subject areas that's so difficult to assess—we can look at a product a student has produced, but it's hard to know what went into it. If you look at a student who is writing, usually all you see is a hand moving or standing still. What is happening inside the mind as that hand is moving? Having students reflect can help us find out, and that in turn helps us make better decisions about how to teach them. Kathie Yancey explains the power of reflection in a writing classroom: "As they learn, they witness their own learning: they show us how they learn" (1998, 8).

REFLECTION BUILDS COMMUNITY

We know that like us, you probably spend a lot of time and energy from the very first day of school striving to build a classroom community where students feel valued, believe they have a voice, know they can take risks, and take ownership of their learning. For us, reflection is a key part of this process. From day one, our students (and their teachers!) are reflecting aloud about who they are as writers, and they have the opportunity to have a conversation as a whole group of writers. During these reflection times, we are careful to emphasize not only what is easy about writing but also what is hard about it. Through reflection, children realize we are all in this together as writers—we share many of the same joys and struggles as we go through the writing process. A community of writers takes shape.

Reflection that helps each student build an identity as a writer in a community of writers begins in the first week of school. As our students are gathered on the rug, Colleen projects and then reads a series of sentence stems for reflection on who we are as writers (see Figure 1.1). As she reads each stem, she and Deana sometimes break into reflection of their own, musing, "I really like writing stories about my family, but I'd like to get better at writing opinions," or "I'm a writer who sometimes

Name _____

I'm a writer who . . .

. . . has written _____

. . . likes to write _____

. . . worries about _____

. . . feels proud of _____

. . . has struggled with _____

. . . wants to try _____

Figure 1.1   Reflective Sentence Stems on Writer Identity

has trouble getting started on a new piece of writing. It's a little scary." We're careful not to overdo it; we've found that while a little modeling helps kids see how to get started, if we model too much then their answers all start to sound like our own.

After she gives directions and allows students an opportunity to ask questions, Colleen simply says, "Off you go!" The children gather up their pencils, papers, and notebooks and move around the room to find a good spot to reflect and write. Hamilton writes that he hopes to publish a book, but he struggles with thinking about what to write next sometimes. Another writer, Jim, pencil flying across paper, jots down his ideas. When a teacher approaches, he eagerly spouts them off: "I wrote a book called 'Sharks' and really like to write comic books, but I worry about Swiss cheese, spiders, and holes." We laugh at this, but we also see how both writers are thinking through who they are as individuals; both are looking at themselves and writing through different lenses.

When it appears most students are finished unpacking their thoughts, Colleen rings the bell to signal it is time to come together again. Sometimes shyly, more often boldly, students begin to share out to the group. As Millie shares that she enjoys writing about animals, other students give a thumbs-up because they feel the same way. As Hamilton talks about how he worries about finishing his stories, some children give a thumbs-up because they, too, have this worry as writers. After a few students have shared, the kids add their papers to their writing notebooks and writing workshop comes to a close.

We value this reflection time right from the first days of school for many reasons, but one big one is the way it brings our writers together in a common challenge. By having the opportunity to reflect and share, students realize they are not alone as writers with successes and struggles.

"It's not just me who likes to write about dogs."

"It's not just me who cannot always figure out what to write next."

"It's not just me who struggles with spelling."

"It's not just me who doesn't know what to write about."

"It's not just me who loves to write fiction."

As we said, sharing not only what is easy but also what is hard helps build community. We see that we all have both different and shared problems. Students move past simply whining about what they are struggling with, or sitting alone with

invitation *to* REFLECT

Teachers can experience the same benefits of reflection as students. Through shared reflection, a group of teachers can move from being neighbors down the hall to being partners in navigating the complex and difficult work of teaching. Even reflecting alone can have this effect on how it feels to teach, for example, when you read and reflect on other teachers' work through their publications (as you are doing right now).

it before a blank page, to knowing themselves as writers who can state struggles in a way that warrants our sincere attention.

REFLECTION BUILDS WRITERS' CONFIDENCE

At the end of writing time one day, Deana announced, "Let's gather on the rug." The second- and third-grade students packed up their pencils and writing notebooks and scurried to the rug to hear a story written by a friend in class. Carrie, notebook clutched in hand, walked to the front of the room, peering out at her audience. After working diligently on developing her ideas, she was eager to share her draft of a twisted fairy tale, a spin on *Little Red Riding Hood* in which a band of well-known superheroes had become the main characters. As she read her fairy tale with expression and vigor, the rest of the class got lost in her words. Robbie giggled at all the right moments. Hye-Su nodded her head as if to say, "Well done; I know that strategy." So far, this was the kind of sharing time you'd find in most any writing workshop, but next, Deana said to the class, "Let's reflect on what you notice Carrie doing as a writer." A smiling Carrie called on her peers to hear what they had to say.

Darren said, "I like the way you carried the story of Little Red Riding Hood through your whole story but made it your own with your own characters. I love superheroes!"

The author, smiling proudly, called on another volunteer. Rachael chimed in, "I like the way you described your characters and included details about what they said or did. It made them come to life for me."

Sharing like this feels good, and kids do learn simply from hearing one another's work. But to us, learning from Carrie's *process* as a writer was even more important. Where did she run into trouble, and from there, how did she find her way to these great narrative moves her classmates were noticing? So Deana gently asked Carrie, "Can you tell about a problem you had in the writing?" Carrie explained that after she had come up with the superheroes idea, she kind of ran out of gas. So superheroes were going through the woods to Grandmother's house . . . what then? A wolf? Seems like they could take care of that pretty easily. The story was kind of boring.

She worked through this problem, she explained, in two ways. With Deana's help, she told how she intentionally gave each superhero details and dialogue, to help readers care about them more as they made their way through the woods. These were the things her classmates had noticed earlier.

"Great thinking, Carrie," remarked Deana. "I love how when you got stuck, instead of dropping your story, you thought about ways to work through it. Sometimes you have to take chances like that."

Writing involves taking many risks. From writing down new and not-yet-formed ideas, to sharing messy drafts, to trying a new writing move that they may not quite have down yet, we are asking our writers to take bold, brave steps almost every time we ask them to write. For this, students need confidence. This isn't necessarily confidence that they can do everything well, but confidence that whatever they try as writers, there is no mistake so bad that it can't be addressed, no idea so bad they can't recover from it. It's the confidence that they have some resources—that they can move through whatever challenges arise in the writing. This confidence is not a false sense of competence; it's assurance that they can write, period, and that if they work on it they can get better.

In this instance, Carrie felt comfortable in her community of writers to take a risk and share her work with the rest of the class, and the others felt comfortable in their community to reflect on what they saw Carrie doing and connect it to their own work. Carrie felt proud of what was accomplished as her peers named specific strategies she used. This boost helped her forward into challenging revisions over the succeeding days. Beyond just helping Carrie, their shared reflection session left all of our writers thinking about what strategies they could also utilize to further develop their own fairy tales. Reflecting together helps kids notice what they have in common, including both successes in their writing and challenges that they can face head-on. Writing is not an easy process. Insights from one writer, like Carrie, are contagious: reflection helps students notice that they do in fact know a lot about writing and do in fact have resources for the hard times that will surely come. They

invitation *to* REFLECT

Teaching can be a discouraging job. It's overwhelming. And when teaching gets overwhelming, it can be tempting to retreat from it, at least on the hard days. Reflection helps with this. Reflective writing and talk can slow down time, helping us to focus mindfully on the moment we're in and the complexity of that one situation (Damico and Whitney 2017) and gain a solid footing for working through it.

Try reflective writing:

◆ When kids are writing, turn to a fresh page in your own notebook and simply observe the class. Who is struggling? Who is writing more than you thought he or she would? What does this room feel like today? What questions bubble up that you can jot down for later? How does this help you feel more on top of the work?

◆ In the time before or after school, spend five minutes writing a brain dump of what you noticed from the day (or the day before). Can you do it once a week? After several weeks, read over your notes and see if there are any patterns.

have seen these problems before, and they have memories of and language for the problems and for some potential solutions. Thus they are confident to press on.

REFLECTION FOSTERS INDEPENDENCE

One of our ultimate goals as teachers is to make ourselves unnecessary. We want kids to grow in independence so that at the start of writing time, we see writers jumping into writing rather than avoiding the blank page. We want kids to grow in independence so that when facing a writing problem, they try to work on it themselves before they come to us. We want them to grow in independence so that when they're happy with something they've written, they call out, "Listen to this!" instead of asking us, "Is this good?"

Reflection helps writers become more independent as they learn to draw on past experiences to meet new challenges. Hye-Su, for example, was working on a persuasive piece of writing about getting a pet guinea pig. She desperately wanted her mother and father's permission to get a pet, but she was unhappy with the introduction to her letter. When Deana stopped by her desk, Hye-Su sighed audibly. "Ugh, I really want a guinea pig, but I hate my introduction."

"Well, Hye-Su, why don't you try to write three different introductions and see which one you like best?"

"Oh, like we did with informational writing? Thanks, Mrs. Washell!" With just this small teaching nudge, Hye-Su was off and running, problem solving and working through the writing process all on her own. She wrote three introductions on a whiteboard and then picked the one she thought would best hook her readers. What Hye-Su had done with our scaffolding in an earlier unit she now did on her own with a one-sentence suggestion.

Reflection also helped Robbie become more independent. Robbie struggled greatly to come up with ideas he thought were worthy of writing. Facing a blank page, he would sigh loudly, put his head down, and drop his pencil listlessly. If he stared at nothing long enough, and made enough noise to distract the kids nearby, eventually a teacher would come by and confer with him. After a month or two of this pattern, Robbie had formed a habit of simply goofing off until a teacher came to help, thereby avoiding the discomfort of getting started altogether. If asked, he had ideas—he was a funny and creative boy!—but the writing process was hard for him. He wanted to be passionately engaged with an idea or he would not write.

Over the course of a school year, Robbie reflected alone, with a teacher, and with classmates about the difficulty he was having. With the class, he also reflected on ways of getting started or getting unstuck; the kids noted together what strategies had worked for them and what hadn't worked as well. He heard classmates—smart friends whom he respected—share that it was hard for them too, and he heard teachers say that they often had the same feelings.

Over time, Robbie realized through reflection that if he just wrote something down, even a bad sentence, then usually something better would come. As time passed, we would still see him motionless before a blank page, but he wasn't waiting for a teacher—and even better, he wasn't creating a diversion to *attract* a teacher. Instead, he was simply thinking about what to do next, considering approaches in his mind until he felt brave enough to try one. Throughout third grade, he spent a lot more time actually writing than he had the previous year. He knew we expected him to work during writing time, but more importantly, he knew when he was likely to have trouble (at the beginning or when he didn't feel invested in the task) and had a range of strategies he was willing to try *without* a teacher. Basically Robbie had transformed as a writer, from one who struggled with unpacking his ideas independently—or even caring to write down any of his ideas at all—to one who saw himself as a writer who had control over his work.

Reflection helps writers learn what to do when there's a problem. More importantly, this knowledge comes from their own experiences, not just from someone telling them what to do.

invitation *to* REFLECT

When you first start teaching writing workshop, or math, or any subject area in a new way or with a new curriculum resource, you probably stick tightly to the book at first. This makes sense; almost all of us will follow a guide closely when doing something new. Most of us, however, will find ways over time to make that guide or resource our own, and branch off from it where appropriate and even replace part of it that seems not to fit our students' needs.

◆ What helps you feel comfortable going off book?
◆ What helps you feel comfortable turning to a resource when you need it?

REFLECTION MAKES WRITING SKILLS TRANSFERABLE

Finally, reflection helps writers build skills that they can use in more than one writing situation. For example, Leticia, a third grader, was working on a piece of fiction about a famous pop star, loosely based on herself. Leticia had many ideas—so many ideas that they went by in rapid-fire succession in her draft. Often she described the actions of the pop star and her friends (dressing for a night out; taking the stage for a big solo; boarding her private jet!) without referencing any of the pronouns, so the reader was left confused about who was doing what. And in her rush to tell the story, Leticia sometimes raced to an event before the previous event was made explicit, then went back to explain, leaving things out of chronological sequence. All this jumping around made Leticia's story really hard to follow.

However, Leticia remembered a strategy she'd used earlier in the year while crafting a piece about how to win a diva singing contest. While that past informational text and this new narrative text were very different, Leticia could see similarities between the problem she'd had then and the problem she was having now. So, she tried a strategy that had worked before: she circled passages in her draft and used numbers to reorder them; then she used stars to indicate places where more detail was needed, adding sentences for those spots on the facing page of her notebook. The result was a story that was much easier to understand—and much more entertaining to the girls in the class she had written it to impress.

This is the kind of revision that reflection makes possible. Reflection makes strategies portable across situations. Donald Schön (1991), a philosopher whose work on reflection is often found in professional development resources for teachers, writes about how building a *repertoire* of practice makes this portability possible. Practicing over time, you gather a set of experiences and ways of describing them. If you accumulate enough of these—have a wide enough repertoire—you get to the point where you can recognize some situations in practice as similar to others. A set of many discrete experiences becomes sets of kinds of experiences. This means you can recognize a situation as a certain kind of situation and then draw on memories of what worked and didn't work in past situations *of this kind* to make a decision about what to do now. Schön calls this "reflective transfer" to the next situation (1995, 97).

And isn't this what we really want for our students: that they learn things about writing that they can use next time, in writing situations beyond our classrooms? Situations that we can't even imagine? Ultimately, we don't care how Leticia's text

invitation *to* REFLECT

Just as reflection helps our writers to see how strategies from one unit or genre might also be useful in a different situation, our own reflection helps us to see how themes and ideas stretch across our many teaching contexts. We see how our work links up across the school day, across the years, or across professional contexts.

- What do you notice about a child in writing workshop that helps you understand her as a learner in math, in social studies, or in science?
- What do you see in this year's class that might be relevant to your teaching next year?

about a pop star, or Carrie's take on *Little Red Riding Hood*, comes out at all. We care about how the writer comes out. We want writers coming out with skills they can transfer to the many writing situations they'll find themselves in next.

Teaching Reflection, Not Just Expecting Reflection

For all of these reasons, we think having students reflect on what they are doing as they write is critically important to their growth as writers. But we also know that reflecting is really hard to do. When we work with fellow teachers, or with secondary school students, we can say, "OK, time for some reflection," and they know what we mean. Thus, we've seen teens and adults write reflection papers after a major writing assignment or have reflective conversations in pairs after an activity, simply because we've asked them to. But when we are working with our second and third graders, just saying, "Reflect!" doesn't work.

We hear this from our colleagues too. "I know reflection is important, but the kids don't know how to do it," one colleague told us.

"Their thoughts just don't seem to dig deep," another said. "Maybe they're not ready."

Other times, it seems to teachers like kids just aren't trying—like they *could* reflect, but they're not working hard enough to reflect. We feel differently. We think young kids can reflect and, once they know what it does for them, usually want to reflect. However, this doesn't mean they know *how* to reflect. We have learned that if we think reflection is important, we need to *teach* reflection, not just *expect* reflection.

HOW DO WE TEACH REFLECTION? THREE KEY COMPONENTS

In our work with our second- and third-grade students, we focus on three key components of reflection. We teach students to

- *remember* what they have practiced;
- *describe* what they have practiced, acquiring metalanguage for talking about writing; and
- *act* upon this information for next time, when writing again.

We consider each of these in detail in the chapters that follow. We show you what each component looks like in action, describe specific strategies we use to teach it, and offer examples and stories from our own students to help you envision what the work might look like in your own classroom. But before we get there, let's consider the three components of reflection in a learning context outside of school.

Anne began learning the piano at the age of forty, and it's been a long, slow road. But reflection is key at every step of her learning. Whether she goes to a lesson, has a practice session at home, or even plays a recital, what does it look like when Anne reflects on these experiences?

Remember

First, we argue, Anne will have to *remember* what she did. This might seem too simple to even write about, but with both kids and adults, remembering can be difficult. Try recounting a conversation you had yesterday. You can probably do it as far as the main ideas go, but will you have them in order? Or will you need to go back and fill in details as you go, realizing you skipped them only when you come to something else that depends on them?

Anne might remember that she practiced this morning, but will she remember what time it was? What pieces she played and in what order? Will she recall just what measures tripped her up? What wrong notes she played? Will she remember what she did when those passages stopped her? Did she start again from the beginning? Replay the tricky spot several times? Play it a time or two with just one hand before trying again with both hands? Did she play the hard measure and then back up a measure and then another? As we were writing this, Anne *had* practiced for a few minutes that morning, but she had a hard time remembering these specifics.

It's the same for kids; they need help remembering what they have done in order to learn from an experience and carry that learning into the future. How many times have you taught something, only to find nobody could recall it at all in the next unit or even the next day? We have helped our students by teaching them specific strategies for remembering both instruction and their own writing experiences. For example, we teach students how to look back through their notebooks and trace the steps of their process (more on this in Chapter 2). When Julie struggled to write a conclusion for an informational piece, she used this strategy and reviewed her notebook to see how she'd worked through conclusions in her earlier writing. We also teach students to use talk as a way to access memories, and Jacob used this strategy as he worked with a small group to think about setting goals in our opinion writing unit. As the group talked about having a meaningful opinion, Jacob remembered a piece of opinion writing from the year before. "I had several reasons, but some of them were obvious. I want to only use the really good ones this time, ones everybody else hasn't already thought of."

For Julie's and Jacob's past writing experiences to be useful to them in this fluid, spontaneous, and unforced way, they first had to remember those experiences. Our goal is that students have ways to help themselves remember, not only when we explicitly prompt them but anytime they need to draw upon past experiences. For this reason, we teach our student writers specific strategies for remembering.

Describe

Second, to reflect on her experience and learn from it, Anne will need to be able to *describe* what she did. When working with the piano teacher, which of these would be more useful?

    a. "I got stuck on measure 73. I played it again and again different ways for a while. That seemed to help."

    b. "When I kept missing the F-sharp in measure 73, I went back and played it hands apart, and then I blocked it. Finally, I tried doubling it. It's much smoother now."

We like example b. By describing specific strategies she used, Anne has a chance to identify which ones worked and to file that information away for next time. What's more, with terms like *hands apart*, *blocking*, and *doubling*, the teacher can help Anne re-create the successful practice during the lesson or can suggest other strategies Anne didn't know to try.

The same is true for our student writers. When they can describe *in specific terms* the problems they had in writing, how they tried to resolve them, and the results of those attempts, they can file that information in their minds for next time as well as share it with teachers and classmates, who can offer further perspective. As you will read later in this book, we work deliberately to help students develop a rich vocabulary of writing process terms. In fact, it's become a competition with some of our students, who have made it their personal mission to notice our use of these words! As we were writing this, in April, anytime we said "revising," our students Zoe and Sean would leap up and shout, "Revising! Ha!" and rush to place a cube in the student jar, signaling a point for the class. Less dramatically but, we think, more importantly, one day when we walked past Maryam and Rachael, we overheard Maryam remarking to her neighbor, "You really persuaded me!" and Rachael explaining, "Well, I spent a lot of time *elaborating* each reason with my *audience* in mind." When kids have words for what they are doing as writers, they can name their actions and share their wisdom with other writers. For this reason, we spend time teaching students how to describe what they do as writers.

Act

Third, we argue, reflection matters only if you use it to *act*. Anne will need to act upon her reflections as a pianist the next time she plays. Otherwise, what's the point of all this remembering and describing? The goal is that the next time she plays, she'll repeat those actions that were successful and avoid those that were unsuccessful.

This is true with student writers as well. When Bethany worked on an informational book this year, she *remembered* the trouble she'd had the year before with a book she'd written on Hanukkah, in which the list of chapters seemed randomly thrown together rather than ordered in any meaningful way. She *described* it to Tara, who was writing about Christmas, using terms like *organize* and *flow*. Then she *acted* on it, not only by helping Tara but by deciding to reorder some chapters in her current draft more logically, to better move from one idea to the next. This is our hope for student writers: that prior learning will inform actions today. We don't want them starting fresh every time—whether it's the next day, the next unit, or the next year. We want students to accumulate rich knowledge about themselves as writers. About what works in different writing situations. About what various problems feel like, where they come from, and what might solve them. And we want students to access and deploy this knowledge in all subsequent instances where it makes sense. We don't leave this learning to chance. We can't just make a new assignment and hope students draw upon their past experiences. We want to be sure they do, so we deliberately teach writers how to act on previous reflections the next time they write.

WHEN DO WE REFLECT?

To teach reflection, we have had to make a commitment to teaching it, a commitment expressed in our use of time. Specifically, we teach reflection intentionally at three different times in our writing workshop: in minilessons or other whole-group teaching, in conferring, and in a weekly dedicated reflection time. While none of these times would likely do much on its own, our aim is that they come together into a coherent focus on reflection as something that's always part of writing.

In minilessons, we try to model reflective thinking anytime we model writing. So, for example, when sharing a draft of something from our own notebooks, we also share some reflection aloud: "Hmmm, let me step back. What am I trying to do here? Let me reflect . . ." That is, we never just write at the board; we always also think aloud about what we're doing in a deliberate and visible way.

In conferring, we also try to model how any time is a good time for reflection. For example, Deana might sit to work with a student who is stuck. "Let's start by remembering," she'll say. "What did you try last time this happened?" She uses the language of *remember*, *describe*, and *act* as she works one-on-one with students, prompting them to make connections between things that happen in whole-class lessons and things that happen in their own notebooks during writing time.

And yet we also find that if we don't set aside deliberate, earmarked time for teaching reflection, we won't get to it, or if we do get to it, we won't teach it as intentionally as we'd hoped. For this reason, we set aside about ten minutes or so every Tuesday after writing workshop as reflection time. It's not a lot of time, but we know *you* know how precious even those ten minutes are in a packed school week. This

invitation *to* REFLECT

◆ The single best source of reflection time for you as a teacher might be where you least expect it: right in the classroom with your students. You've heard it before: *write along with your students.* When kids write, we write notes about students that we want to remember, or we reflect for just a moment on something we'll pick up and think more about later.

◆ Kim Stafford writes in "Quilting Your Little Solitudes: How to Write When You Don't Have Time To" (1996) about finding microperiods of time that can add up to something significant. Maybe you sit for thirty minutes in the steamy natatorium, waiting while a child has a swimming lesson, like Anne does. Or maybe you can fit in ten minutes before you turn on your computer in the morning. One teacher we know dictates reflections to herself using the recorder on her phone while driving home from work. Then, when something is really troubling her, she goes back and listens to a few of those recordings with a mind for noticing important themes or recurring ideas.

is different from the typical share time at the end of a writing workshop; this time isn't about sharing the writing itself so much as sharing about how the writing felt, what processes students used, and what we learned as writers from doing it. You'll see how we use those minutes—what we do, how students respond, what we say, and what kids write—all through the rest of this book.

Looking Forward: Where Reflection Leads Us

Our second- and third-grade classrooms are likely very much like yours. We have a range of diverse students with diverse needs, we have huge amounts of content to teach, and we never, ever seem to have enough time. When we first began to focus together on helping students build strong identities as writers, it was hard enough to even make time for writing at all. And when we began to add reflection into the mix, it got even more daunting. Yet because it is important to us, we have persisted, and over time we are seeing a change in our students as writers.

Remember Robbie, who had trouble getting started and had become dependent on a teacher to help him begin to write? Reflecting together on our work with him, we realized that in all the writing he had done that year, either we or his parents were pushing him forward. *We* were doing too much of the work. Instead, we wanted Robbie to notice how he felt when it was time to write. What was making it difficult? And in those moments when he did write, what made that feel worth doing? This is where reflection came in. In conferring with him, we started asking questions like these. And with the class as a whole, we began to emphasize strategies for reflection.

At the end of the year, Robbie seemed to understand more of who he was as a writer, and he knew how to put that knowledge to work. Our previous image of him had been of a boy rolling on the floor, getting up to sharpen a pencil, or crumpling papers and tossing them from his desk. Now we're more likely to picture him as the proud author of a narrative about a teacher who had a magic pencil. Focused with determination, he owned that story! Pencil flying across the paper, sitting upright in his desk, he was thoughtful in what ideas he included. When a teacher offered help as he prepared to publish, he assured us that this writing was indeed his and he had his narrative "under control"—his control.

We're not miracle workers, but we have seen changes like these in many of our writers as we've both increased the choice and responsibility they've had for their work and taught them very deliberately how to reflect actively. Reflection helps students to know what they are doing in writing and why—and thus to learn from what they are doing. Where once we sometimes felt like we were dragging kids through a series of writing units, now it's more often the case that we're scrambling to add time to our writing plans because the kids have more they want to do. While we still have the full range of writers, from reluctant to eager, many of our former tough cookies are now our most avid writers. And we see results not only in their willingness but also in the texts that they produce.

chapter

TWO

Writers Remember

Early in our work in learning how to help students build strong identities as writers, we came to the end of a unit and were preparing for a publication celebration. Students had started several personal narratives, using a range of strategies for invention we had taught in minilessons. They each had selected one narrative to take to completion, and they had engaged in several days of revising, including getting a partner's feedback, adding detail to their drafts, thinking about organization, and adding dialogue. As they were editing, making final copies, and illustrating finished pieces for inclusion in a class book, we decided to have our students reflect on the process. While we had used reflection here and there along the way, this was one of the first times we had set aside deliberate carpet time for it and planned for a whole-group reflective conversation.

"What are some of the things we worked on in writing workshop that helped you get your draft to this point?" we asked the class.

Nothing. Our usually boisterous students sat silently, picking at their shoelaces.

But, we are experienced teachers with good wait time, so we waited. Still nothing. Finally, a few hands went up from those good little participants who always raised their hands and tried hard to do what we were asking.

"I made my story better."

"I fixed the things that were wrong in my story."

"My partner helped me make my story better."

What was happening? These were not the reflective responses we'd expected from this smart, engaged group of second- and third-grade writers. We had expected detailed accounts of decisions made along the way to a final draft: endings written and then discarded, paragraphs reordered, helpful encounters with a partner's clarifying questions. Instead, we just got "I made it better."

We were stumped, and (if we're honest) maybe a little disappointed with our students. As we debriefed, we wondered: "Was this over their heads? They can reflect on things they've read; why not on their writing? Have they even been with us through all these weeks of workshop?"

We realized that when we asked about a specific classroom activity or a specific strategy we had taught, our students could talk easily about it; it was the open-ended invitation to draw from multiple experiences over a long period of time that they struggled with. It wasn't exactly that they couldn't reflect; it was that they couldn't necessarily *remember* what we had been doing in order to reflect upon it. After all, these were second and third graders: they didn't necessarily know what day of the week it was, and they got this morning confused with last week. Or, they could remember things we had done in class when prompted a bit, but the memories weren't necessarily organized in their minds in ways that they could surface and scroll through themselves.

Remembering Connects Us to Identity

As adults, when we engage in an activity that we own as part of our identity—like running, quilting, or gardening, for instance—we remember important experiences we've had as a runner, a quilter, or a gardener over time. For example, Anne sings in a choir. When she's in that role, she draws in part on her memories and the lessons she's learned from the many, many previous times she has sung with a choir, from the bit parts she had in elementary school musicals, to the time she blew a big audition in high school, to the solo she sang on Christmas Eve in a sanctuary lit by flickering candlelight. These are more than nice memories for the photo album; they are tools Anne can and does draw upon for singing now. That bad audition, along with the time Anne has thought about it and talked about it in the years since, is right with her in the present every time she takes calming breaths to steady her nerves before singing. The memory of that Christmas Eve emboldens Anne to try newer and more challenging solos that she might otherwise shy away from: "Well, this is hard, but when I did that other scary Christmas solo it felt amazing afterward, and having memorized my piece really helped me feel secure. I think I'll try again."

The same is true with writing. As an adult writer, you probably remember many writing experiences you've had, and those memories inform your current writing. You remember how, when you finally learned in your last year of college to start papers right away instead of the night before they were due, you realized that "I write best under pressure" wasn't exactly true for you—it was that you had been using pressure to force yourself to write at all. Now you draw on that discovery to schedule writing time when you know a deadline approaches.

You remember all the times you've accidentally hit Send on an email, only to notice a typo just as you've heard the "whoosh" of that message going right to someone whose opinion you cared about, and you draw on that memory to proofread something carefully when you know it's really important.

You remember when someone showed you a helpful organizing strategy for a piece of writing, and now you sometimes use it—but not just anytime. You use it when the writing situation you're facing reminds you of a situation where the strategy was helpful.

Remembering the decisions you made as a writer, and the outcomes those decisions produced, is a prerequisite for getting better at making those decisions in the future. And over time you learn to say, "I'm a writer who needs to plan ahead," or "I'm a writer who works well from an outline," or "I'm a writer who needs to talk it out before writing," or "I'm a writer who can miss a lot of typos if I'm not careful." Note that all of those statements start with "I'm a writer who . . . ," an agentive claim of identity that is key to getting better and growing stronger.

If our students couldn't remember what they had been doing with their writing, or if they couldn't put their memories together into a kind of story about how they had handled a piece of writing, then how could they say they were writers? How could they tap the strength that would come from knowing themselves in that particular way? We could call them *writers* all day long, but it would be nothing more than a cute label if they had no memories in which to ground their identities.

Over time we've come to understand that we need to scaffold remembering as part of a process of reflection. Our students need clear and reliable memories of their writing experiences to think about, talk about, learn from, and draw upon each time they write. They need writing experiences that are truly theirs so they can eventually say, "I'm a writer who . . . ," and have those words mean something.

Teaching Remembering

When we say we teach students to *remember*, we mean we support students as they recall and retell—with specificity—what happened in their writing practice. We find it helpful to have students focus on three specific kinds of remembering:

1. Remembering *what* was taught and *what* they did in their writing

2. Remembering *how* they did it and the results

3. Remembering *why* they did it

With this framework in mind, we plan engagements that help students learn to remember their actions so reflection becomes possible. Next, we consider the purpose of each kind of remembering, and then we share some of the most powerful engagements we've developed to support our students in remembering.

REMEMBERING *WHAT*

In order to reflect, students need to recall both the writing experiences they shared and those they experienced as individuals. That seems obvious enough, but writers need support to remember specifics: What did we (the teachers) teach in minilessons and conferences—and how many times did we teach it? What anchor charts did the class make and use? What did the students do? What strategies did they use? What decisions and choices did they make? What texts did they refer to as models? What did the class talk about during share times? In other words, at a basic level, *what happened?*

Since our ultimate goal is for students to build strong identities as writers through reflection, remembering experiences is really important. In his book *Choice Words* (2004), Peter Johnston describes how the stories we position students to tell about themselves have consequences for their academic identities. When we ask a student a question like "What did you do today as a writer?" we create a space in which it is presumed that (a) the student is a writer, a real one; (b) the student is *doing* things, actively, when writing; and (c) the writer is doing these things with intention, usually to make the piece of writing better. As Johnston explains, these assumptions "[make] it hard for the student to reject either the identity or the action. . . . The student is gently nudged—well, all right, pushed—to rehearse a narrative with herself as the writer/protagonist" (26).

Our teaching needs to position students not just as authors of the texts they write but also as authors of stories of their own processes and development as writers. To develop strong identities, students need to be able to tell stories about themselves *as writers* where they are the main characters—the protagonists—who make the decisions and take the actions that lead to the production of a written text. As they learn to tell these stories with specific, chronological detail, the practices we suggest become more than just things to do because a teacher has asked for it; they become possible additions to students' own repertoires of practice.

REMEMBERING *HOW*

If remembering *what* they did helps students tell stories about themselves as writers, remembering *how* they did things adds important detail to those stories. Most of remembering *how* is procedural knowledge: What were the steps? What materials were used? How did it turn out? And, perhaps most importantly, what would you have to do in order to do it again? For example, if Jack remembered that he made a new lead for his narrative (that's the *what*), then remembering *how* would involve recalling that a teacher modeled writing three kinds of leads, that he looked in picture books to see more examples, that he experimented with a few, and that a partner helped him choose which one seemed most effective to her as a reader.

REMEMBERING *WHY*

Finally, students need to remember *why* they did what they did as writers. What was the context or situation that led the writer to make this decision or take this action? For example, let's say Marianna is practicing writing dialogue for characters in her narrative. Why? Did she get feedback that her story was boring? Did she think it might offer insight into the characters? Was she attending closely to a minilesson about dialogue? Did she get the idea from a book she was reading? *Why?*

When we say remembering *why*, we are really referring to the whole array of conditional and contextual knowledge that surrounds a writing experience and impacts decision making: What was happening? What was important at the time? What audience was involved? What teachers or partners played a role? Asking someone why they did something presumes that they had reasons, *good* reasons. It presumes intention. And then it's on the students to think about what their intentions were in a particular moment.

REMEMBERING THAT DECISION-MAKING MATTERS

We're mindful that asking questions about *what*, *how*, and *why* is really most powerful only when students are making the decisions about what they do. For many students, this kind of decision making is rare. Too often, the presumption in school is that students do things simply because they are told to, for no purpose other than that they are at school, and "at school we do school."

As you'll see in the strategies we offer next, we do care that students remember the "doing school" part of what we taught and what they did as a class. But just as important, if not more so, are students' memories about specific things they *chose* to try and how those experiments went. We want to know the following:

- Whom did you go to for feedback, and what (and how helpful) was the feedback?

- When a teacher offered choices about how to begin a story, which one did you pick, and with what outcome?

- What process did you go through to move from ideas and starts of drafts to a story idea you were willing to carry forward through revision?

- Where did you take a risk?

Questions like these position students to own and tell their stories about what they do as writers, which, in turn, makes them intentional and powerful authors of their identities as writers. Students can learn not only from their own remembering (and the examination of those memories, which comes after) but from the remembering work of others. When they share stories and compare notes, they add to their internal list of possibilities for next time, and they get a sense of the many right ways to do a thing. But this benefit is possible only when the stories are truly the students' own and are as varied as the many different decisions individual writers inevitably make.

Strategies for Remembering

How do you remember important things that have happened? What strategies do you use to make sure you can access your memories when you need them? We know there are many ways people help themselves remember, but we also know we probably use some of the same strategies you do: we take and keep photos, make notes for next time, write in journals, and talk with people when important things happen. These are the same basic strategies we teach our students to use again and again throughout the year to help them remember and then reflect on their experiences in writing workshop. Through these shared strategies, students develop habits they can use independently for more effective individual reflection.

In the sections that follow, we highlight four of the most important remembering strategies we use: (1) the time line; (2) the notebook flip; (3) the table of contents; and (4) photo or video elicitation. For each strategy, we offer a snapshot of how it works with our students, and then we step back and think through why we do it, what it makes possible, and how you might adapt the strategy to use with students in your own context.

TIME LINE

The time line strategy is useful for helping students remember their shared experiences along a sequence of instruction. For example, if we took the whole class through three different experiments with organizing a piece of writing, and then we wanted them to reflect on the decisions they ultimately made about organizing their own pieces, then we would need to help them remember what the three experiments were before much else could happen.

Snapshot of the Time Line in Action

We gather the class on the carpet and tape a long, horizontal sheet of butcher paper to the board. We will be referring to the time line later, so we want a paper copy that we can keep on the wall. We draw a horizontal line across the paper, representing linear time (though we don't say anything explicit about that to start). We set the scene for the class quite simply: "Along the way to these narratives we're finishing, we've done a lot of things as a class. What are some of the things we've done?"

Students begin to raise hands, and when we see hands from about half the class, we start to take input.

"We drew those lands," one child offers.

"Those maps!" clarifies another. And we write "territory maps" on our time line, leaving some space before and after for other things we taught.

"We're doing our illustrations," someone adds, and we write that to the far right of our line. We just started to add illustrations the day before, and only those students with a fairly solid written draft are adding them at this point.

Another student struggles to add his recollection: "There was that day . . . you screamed . . . pajama day . . ."

Friends jump in: "You dropped the book! We wrote about it!"

They are referring to an exercise in vivid diction. One day, Anne entered the classroom reading a book and bumped into someone on her way, knocking over a tin of blocks. She looked up in surprise as the blocks clattered onto the floor. That's when she saw that the students were in pajamas. "What!?" Anne cried. "Why didn't anybody tell me it was pajama day?" She threw her book to the side in disgust and hurried out of the room in a huff. Before the kids could talk about what they had just seen, Colleen and Deana directed them *not* to talk about it, but to write about it. After they did, they compared what they had written to see the broad range of word choices available for describing any one scene.

We write this memory on the time line as "vivid language." Using our own teaching vocabulary and not the students' words is a deliberate choice; we think it's important to help students know and use precise terms to describe what they do as writers. (We will dig into this in detail in the next chapter.)

Continuing the time line, one by one, students recall and we record in rough chronological order the other strategies we have taught over the past few weeks: finding a good spot to work in, choosing a piece of writing to develop further, using a storyteller voice, crafting leads.

Before long, our time line is full (See Figure 2.1 for examples of time lines for other genres.). Students begin to comment on it without prompting:

"We've done a lot!"

"I forgot we had done some of those."

"It takes a lot to finish a piece of writing."

We leave the time line up on the wall until we have published our narratives in a class book and read-around. We're not just here to write narratives (or informational books, or letters, or essays); we are here to become writers. This time line is evidence; it's like a trail of bread crumbs tracing our journey.

Unpacking the Time Line Strategy

One reason we engage students in making the time line is simply to mirror back to them—and honor and celebrate—all of the hard work that went into the completion of a finished piece of writing. One experience many students have in school is that once they've finally mastered something difficult, they look up from their work to find that others in the class have now moved far ahead. It's like a bike ride Anne remembers having with a partner who was more fit than her. At the top of a big hill, this friend would kindly wait for Anne to reach the top too, but then he would immediately resume riding as Anne came up the crest. He was not only in better shape

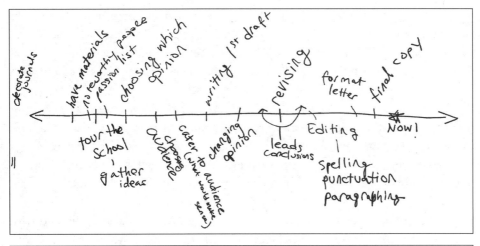

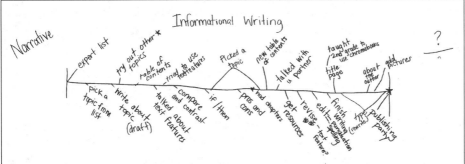

Figure 2.1   Completed Time Lines

but had also had a nice break while waiting for Anne to reach the top; when Anne arrived huffing and puffing, she got no break at all if she was going to avoid falling behind again. This was discouraging! While every writer in the room is climbing different hills at different paces, we think it's important to stop and spend some time together at the top, noticing the different things writers have done to get there.

Second, as the students co-create the time line, it allows them to take ownership of the work they did as writers. In our classroom, while we value opportunities for choice and strive to position students as independently as possible, we do have a district-adopted curriculum resource in place and we do work together through units of study, typically specifying at least in part the genres students will write and when they are due to be finished. In addition to these constraints on student choice, of course, we also teach specific whole-class minilessons as we see the needs of the class developing. This means it's possible, if we're not careful, for students to see the narrative trajectory of our writing workshop as a series of actions the teachers took instead of as a series of actions they took: "She taught us about leads. She taught us about gathering ideas. She showed us how to punctuate dialogue," and so on. And yes, we *do* do all those things as teachers! Yet we want students' memories of writing—and their subsequent reflection—to be memories of things they did with intention and from which they experienced results.

If students are to own the memories of their work in the study, it's important that *they* recall what happened and organize it all in their memory. We could have easily created a time line over the course of our narrative study by adding a strategy each day we introduced one, but that would have been us doing the work, with us as protagonists in the story of writing development. The time line would have been just another anchor chart used at the end of the unit instead of a useful document for reflection that students made out of their own sense of what they did and why. And indeed, making it themselves helped them become meaningfully engaged with the reflection process. As our second and third graders gazed upon the huge time line plastered across the front of the room, watching it get more and more crowded with things they remembered doing (things they remembered struggling with, liking, finding useful, or even trying and rejecting), their faces lit up, their minds locked in, and hands shot up as students built upon one another's responses.

Once a time line is up in front of the class and most students feel it's complete, we look at it together and talk. We usually start with "What do you notice about this?" With some classes, this is enough! Someone will notice that several of the items on the time line involve partner work. "Great observation," we say, and then we ask, "What's something you learned about writing from a partner this unit? Can you turn and talk to someone near you about that?" Here are some questions you might ask writers about a time line:

- ◆ What work did we do that was most helpful to you as a writer?
- ◆ What work do you see on this time line that you've done many times before? And what work do you see up here that was new for you this time?
- ◆ Where on this time line did you have the most energy?
- ◆ Where did you struggle with the work?
- ◆ What on this time line are you especially proud of?
- ◆ What on this time line do you really want to incorporate into your next major piece of writing?

Questions like these take students from remembering to reflecting more thoroughly on what they have remembered. There's so much more to think about once those memories are all laid out for the writers to see.

invitation *to* REFLECT

Try using a time line to provoke reflection of your own. First, choose some period of time that you want to reflect on. It might be a time line of one of these events, for example:

- ◆ your experiences with using a new curriculum resource
- ◆ your experiences with a particular student you'd like to understand better
- ◆ your journey in a strand of professional development—perhaps National Board certification, the National Writing Project, a master's degree program, or a professional community you've joined
- ◆ your school year after switching to a new grade level or school building

Next, spend some time simply making the time line. Stop yourself from trying to make a beautiful drawing or fitting it all elegantly onto your paper. Stay focused on generating ideas.

Once you've got your time line, you can think about it the same way you would ask your students to do. Here are some questions you might ask yourself:

- ◆ Are any events repeated or similar to one another? In what way(s)? Is this intentional, or is it that something keeps recurring whether I like it or not?
- ◆ What themes emerge here?
- ◆ What emotions accompany the events? How are those contributing in positive and negative ways to what is happening? Are there triggers here that stop me from learning or accomplishing my goals? Are there sparks that energize or inspire me— and if so, could I make those happen more often?
- ◆ Where on the time line are significant learning events, for me or my students? What led up to those? Are there any common sequences or steps that I could take more deliberately in the future?
- ◆ What other people show up on the time line? Who is influencing me? Which of these influences might I nurture and increase? Are there any influences I need to take steps to minimize?

You might think about using this same strategy in your own classroom as a way to wrap up a unit of writing—or work over time in *any* content area. Co-constructed time lines allow students to be proud not just of a finished product but also of all the work they did to get to that product. Time lines emphasize process rather than product and position the finished work as just one of many artifacts of the journey taken to get there.

NOTEBOOK FLIP

Similar to the time line, the notebook flip is about creating a shared list of activities and strategies students have learned and used. But while the time line is a shared experience where we simply think back to remember, with the notebook flip, students ground their remembering in the artifacts they find in their notebooks. Over time, we want student writers to be able to remember and reflect independently—so even though we also do the notebook flip as a shared activity, when students use their own work as a prompt for remembering, they are moving toward more independent reflection.

For the notebook flip, we use the familiar routine and vocabulary of the daily schedule as a scaffold to help students remember their writing processes. To preview the day's schedule each morning, Colleen's class uses a pocket chart featuring cards with ordinal and transition words: "First we have . . . ," "Later we have . . . ," "Subsequently we have . . . ," "After that . . . ," and so on. These words help children order the actions they see they've taken in their notebooks in meaningful ways.

Snapshot of the Notebook Flip in Action

Our students are gathered on the rug with their notebooks in their laps.

"Look in your notebooks. What is one thing you have done as you worked on your writing so far?" We wait for many hands to go up before asking for responses.

"Territory map," a student offers. We write this on a pink card.

"OK, we'll place that here for now. We can move it if we need to," we say and stick it in a pocket.

More card suggestions come.

"We made writing goals."

"We worked with a partner."

"We wrote whatever stories we wanted."

"I made a new story from my school map."

Some are shared actions, things we asked all students to try; others are decisions that individual writers have made on their own. We value both, but our main focus in this notebook flip is to highlight the progression of all the things we have done together. Along the way, we remark, "Yes, many of us tried that," or "Yes, we had a whole-class lesson on that." We write each response on a pink card and place it, with students' help, into a pocket; we shift other cards around as students decide upon the order. Figure 2.2 shows the result.

Figure 2.2 Completed Notebook Flip

Unpacking the Notebook Flip

When we teach students to remember, ordering events is important. No, it's not terribly important that students be able to recall an entire calendar of instruction. We wouldn't expect them to remember in a music class that they learned quarter notes on September 5, half notes on September 12, whole notes on September 19, *piano* and *forte* on September 26, and crescendos on October 3. But we would want students to know they learned to read some notes and the names and values of those notes. We would want them to realize that they know some dynamics—and to have the word *dynamics*. And we would want them to know how they moved from shorter notes to longer ones, or from single words for soft and loud to the more complex notion of crescendos—notes or phrases that increase in volume—after that.

The key is, we want students not only to remember individual things they learned but also to have a sense of how they fit together, how they form a progression. It's not simply that things happened in an order: "First this; then that." It's that events led to one another and are connected to cumulative ends: "I did this, then that, and so I decided to do that." Or "I noticed this, so I did this, and then that helped me see that." Way leads on to way in developing a piece of writing, so when we help students look back, recall, and order events, we are also helping them to see the links between those events.

When writers can see that they have engaged in a meaningful arc of connected experiences leading to both a written product *and* some expertise, they can carry that expertise forward beyond that product. Students realize through reflection that writers go through a process and that as they do work, they gain knowledge and resources in a cumulative way. The more they try, the more they have and can use going forward. Naming experiences and ordering them make students aware of that arc and the relationships (not only chronological but more substantive relationships) of the experiences along the way.

Because remembering is prompted by students actually looking at an artifact of their practice, actions that only *some* students have taken make their way onto the notebook flip board. Other students see those actions and, we hope, acknowledge them as possible paths they might have taken but didn't. This is why the negotiations about the order of the cards and what labels might go on the pockets are so important (and thus why we do this together instead of individually). For some students, it's that sharing with a partner led to revising a story's lead. For other students, it's that sharing with a partner led to a new idea for a story or that revising a lead led the writer to seek out a partner for further feedback. Because we have a single pocket chart for the class, we can moderate the discussion about where things might go, and while we do eventually choose just one pocket in which to place each card, we do it in a way that shows the placement is just one of many possibilities: "I'm going to stick this one here for now because it seems to fit for a lot of people, but everyone has a different experience," we say.

Another important aspect of the notebook flip is that students come to view the notebook as an important record of practice and as a useful tool worth their attention. As an adult, it would probably be natural that if you wanted to remember how you did something, you'd look back at your notes. But for a student writer having his or her own notebook for the very first time, that's a new process. Up until second grade, most students probably haven't had record-keeping systems of their own or had any responsibility for maintaining folders of their work—a teacher has taken care of all that. Now, our students have both a writing notebook and a writing binder. The writing notebook is a composition book students have decorated that contains all kinds of idea gathering and drafting. Many of our students have not learned to reliably write the date, and they may not even start pieces of writing on the next available page, so the notebook may or may not be chronologically arranged.

When students sit on the rug and search their notebooks for moves they can have us write on the cards, they are learning that their notebooks contain evidence of their practice. When they notice differences between their notebooks and those of other students, they are also coming to *own* their notebooks as unique artifacts of their own writing processes, rather than simply as administrative structures set up by teachers (structures that they spend a *lot* of school time interacting with).

The notebook flip is a strategy you might use with any unit of study—in any content area—where you are asking students to collect information, gather artifacts, or keep notebooks. For example, when we finish a unit of study in science, we ask our students to look back over their science notebooks and notice their learning, and then we base classroom conversations on what students find as they search. When we want to make students' work visible or help them connect the links in their learning, we work together and use this strategy to name and order what they have done.

Once the notebook flip chart is there, you have something concrete to talk about for broader reflection. Try questions like these:

◆ What do you notice about this? (We know this question is vague, but we like to start here. Students try so hard to anticipate what we are looking for; a very open question like this can be generative of students' ideas that we hadn't even considered.)

- What differences do you notice between your notebook process and a neighbor's? What explains those differences?

- What was most helpful?

- What did you try that was not so helpful? Is there a different way of doing it that might have been *more* helpful?

- How is this similar to or different from other notebook flips? (if you're doing the notebook flip for the second or third time with a class)

A NOTE ON NOTEBOOKS

We used to use single composition notebooks for writing that lasted all year. Students decorated them at the beginning of the year with personal mementos, and notebooks included idea-generating pieces such as heart maps and neighborhood maps that students would refer back to all year. Our students felt real ownership of these notebooks, but in a lot of ways, they were just not the best tool for them as writers.

For one thing, the lines in the notebooks were too small for most of our writers. And then there was the problem of organization. Some students were more organized and used the notebooks sequentially, but with many others, writing was happening all over the notebook and it wasn't in chronological order. Some students seemed to open randomly to the middle to start new entries, and they would often lose track of this writing somewhere within the thick notebook. And when notebooks would mysteriously get lost, as they sometimes do, a whole year's worth of work would be lost too.

There is always a balance to be struck between keeping things organized and keeping student work, not organization, at the center of attention. As we reflected on this challenge, we decided to shift to using thin notebooks that we change with each new unit of study or when a notebook is filled, whichever comes first. These come in a range of line styles and widths, so that we can support students in successful handwriting (which also makes navigating the notebook easier). They're thin, so even when students start new entries on random middle pages, they are able to find them easily. And when students begin a new notebook, we store the old one, which is helpful to us in our own and our students' assessment of their growth over time (see Chapter 5 for more on this).

NOTEBOOK TABLE OF CONTENTS

As students get better at remembering, first from shared oral reflection (time line) and then from the collaborative mining of individual experiences and artifacts (notebook flip), we can move from whole-class strategies for remembering to more individualized strategies. One way is to have students analyze their notebooks in more depth: what steps have brought them to where they are now? Yet as we mentioned, for our students, the notebook itself can be hard to navigate.

Without a whole lot of scaffolding from us, students may just open to any page and start writing—which is fine if all they need is a piece of paper. But it becomes difficult later on when they can't find what they've written or have pages of a multiple-page stoyy in different places scattered throughout the notebook. We have them mark important things, such as the piece of writing they plan to return to for the next day, with stickies, yet if too many days go by, they may not remember what those stickies indicate, even if they are labeled. Their notebook pages are usually not dated, though we've tried with varying amounts of success to instill this as a habit at different times. Handouts and writing paper we hand to kids, such as primary paper, comic paper, or paper for illustrating, may or may not find their way into binders, and the tabs in those binders may or may not be meaningful to kids.

The bottom line is, what good is a notebook if you can't find things in it? In order for children to better utilize their notebooks as a tool for remembering, we scaffold their organization using a table-of-contents strategy that helps them put things in order as they revisit past work.

Snapshot of the Table of Contents in Action

After students have been working in notebooks for a while, we hand out a sheet like the one in Figure 2.3. Students use this to make a rough table of contents for their notebook, or perhaps just for some section of the notebook that we have marked off for them, such as from the beginning of a unit of study. Beginning at the beginning, they identify chunks or chapters of notebook content, briefly note what that content is on the left side of the chart, and then give a page number in the right-hand column.

In cases where numbering the pages is just too difficult, another way is to use different-colored tape flags or stickies to mark off each chunk and then put color codes into the "Page" column. In our experiences, though, sticky notes aren't durable enough to withstand second- and third-grade treatment for long, so while we may do color codes for particular students who need it, with the class as a whole we aim toward page numbering. There is a hope, too, that down the road page numbering might become a habit—and, for Bullet Journal enthusiasts, so might the notion of a running table of contents (see http://bulletjournal.com/ for more on Bullet Journals, a notebook-keeping strategy popular among many of the adults we know).

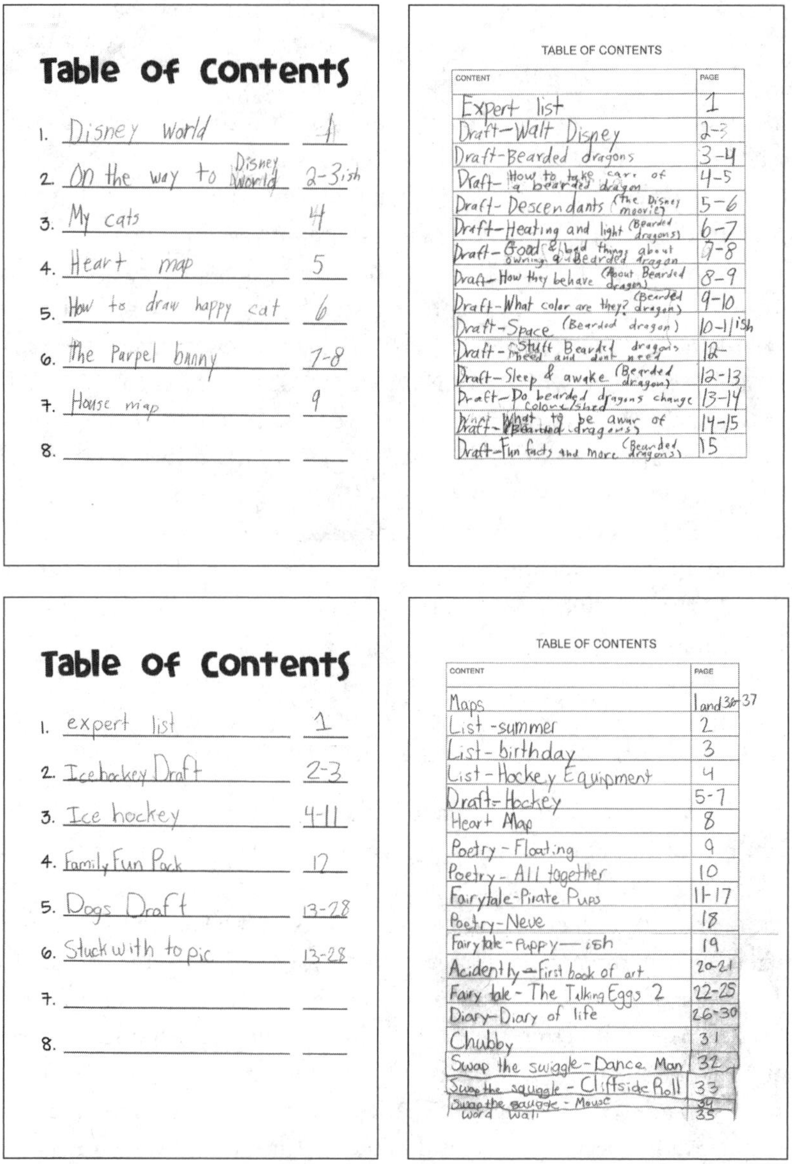

Table of Contents

1.	Disney World	1
2.	On the way to Disney World	2-3ish
3.	My cats	4
4.	Heart map	5
5.	How to draw happy cat	6
6.	The Parpel bunny	7-8
7.	House map	9
8.		

TABLE OF CONTENTS

CONTENT	PAGE
Expert list	1
Draft—Walt Disney	2-3
Draft-Bearded dragons	3-4
Draft- How to take care of a bearded dragon	4-5
Draft- Descendants (the Disney moovie)	5-6
Draft—Heating and light (Bearded dragons)	6-7
Draft—Good & bad things about owning a Bearded dragon	7-8
Draft—How they behave (About Bearded dragons)	8-9
Draft—What color are they? (Bearded dragons)	9-10
Draft-Space (Bearded dragon)	10-11ish
Draft-Stuff Bearded dragons need and don't need	12-
Draft-Sleep & awake (Bearded dragons)	12-13
Draft—Do bearded dragons change colors/shed	13-14
Draft-What to be awar of [illegible] dragons	14-15
Draft—Fun facts and more (Bearded dragons)	15

Table of Contents

1.	expert list	1
2.	Icehockey Draft	2-3
3.	Ice hockey	4-11
4.	Family Fun Pack	12
5.	Dogs Draft	13-28
6.	Stuck with topic	13-28
7.		
8.		

TABLE OF CONTENTS

CONTENT	PAGE
Maps	1 and 36-37
List -summer	2
List- birthday	3
List-Hockey Equipment	4
Draft-Hockey	5-7
Heart Map	8
Poetry - Floating	9
Poetry - All together	10
Fairytale-Pirate Pups	11-17
Poetry-Neve	18
Fairy tale - Puppy—ish	19
Acidently—First book of art	20-21
Fairy tale - The Talking Eggs 2	22-25
Diary-Diary of life	26-30
Chubby	31
Swap the swiggle - Dance Man	32
Swap the squiggle - Cliffside Roll	33
Swap the squiggle - Mouse	34
Word Wall	35

Figure 2.3 Notebook Table-of-Contents Sheet and Completed Examples

Unpacking the Table of Contents

This strategy helps students understand their work in thematic terms, and our use of the word *chunk* to describe what might go in a table of contents is deliberate. Chunks of writing in a notebook are defined by students, and their boundaries are meaningful and visible to students. Simply going day by day would obscure how writers can and do work on single tasks over periods of time longer than a day or on more than one task in a day—goals we have for many of our student writers as their texts get longer and their investment deepens. Likewise, while a lesson-by-lesson way of identifying contents might make sense to us, the ones who plan and teach the lessons, we have to admit that not every lesson we teach reflects a great milestone in a student's piece of writing. Some of our minilessons just don't play into every writer's piece in a big way at that particular time. Other times multiple minilessons arrange themselves into a single chunk in the life of a writer and a piece of writing. So, for example, one student might list "look at house map" and "talk to Naomi" as two separate events, while another student might list those together in a chunk she names "getting ideas." When we see a move like that, we see that this student is thinking deeply about her process, seeing how different actions worked together to create an arc of experiences as she developed her text.

Deciding for themselves where the boundaries are for particular steps in their writing process means claiming that they have engaged in a process, period. It means thinking about what the important steps in the process have been and giving those steps names in the left-hand column. It means remembering all of the work that went into the development of a piece of writing.

The chunking that students do in a table of contents is an important new move in how they remember their work on a piece of writing. The time line helps students learn to identify events in a shared writing process and arrange them in sequence. The notebook flip teaches students to identify events in shared and individual writing processes and link them connectively. The table of contents adds the categorizing or grouping of linked events. By grouping events in their writing process, students don't just come to remember single, disparate actions in a writing process but also see them as *kinds* of actions (categorizing) and amalgamate them into episodes or chapters in the story of their work on a piece of writing.

Once your students have a table of contents, you might want to use that as a starter for a conversation—as a whole group, with a small group, or even with an individual student in a conference. Here are some questions you and your writers could use to learn from their tables of contents. These require some abstract thinking, so you'll need to judge what will fit your own class most appropriately.

◆ In which chunk or chapter of work did you have to work the hardest? What was tough about it? How did you handle it?

◆ Are there chunks or chapters here that turned out not to make it into your final draft? Why not? And what did you learn from doing that work, even if it didn't make it into the published writing?

◆ Which of these chunks or chapters are specific to narrative writing [or whatever genre the writer has been working in]? Which would probably be there for *any* genre of writing?

◆ Let's find some books in the classroom that have a table of contents. See how some of these have just a list of chapters, but others have Part 1, Part 2, and so on, with a few chapters grouped under each part? What would your Part 1, Part 2, and Part 3 be? Which chapters could you group together under a shared main idea?

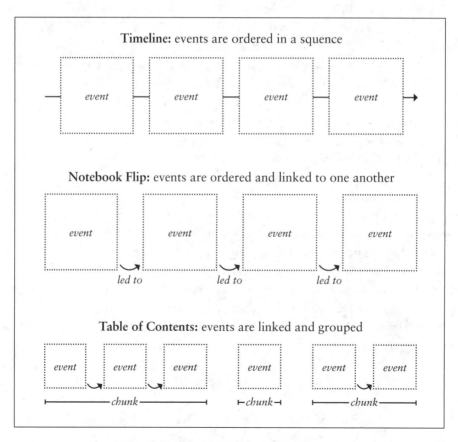

Figure 2.4 Comparison of Strategies for Remembering

As you work with notebook tables of contents, make sure students understand that it's not a table of contents for a finished piece of writing; it's a table of contents for all the work that went into that finished piece. The goal here is to document a process and then think about it, not simply to describe how a product is organized. In talking about this with kids, it might be helpful to refer to those videos on a DVD that chronicle the making of the feature film. What are the different phases that went into the making of their piece of writing?

PHOTO ELICITATION

Finally, we have borrowed the strategy of photo elicitation from our past experiences with teacher inquiry and research. In research, elicitation is the practice of using an artifact to get people remembering and talking. For example, if interviewing a teacher about events in her career, Anne might bring photos of the teacher's former students to help her remember specific people and events of the past. The photos elicit the memories.

Luckily, in classrooms today, photos are incredibly easy to take, edit, organize, project for viewing, and share; they're the perfect tools for remembering and reflection. You can use photos in myriad ways to elicit powerful thinking from your students.

Snapshot of Photo Elicitation in Action

After a minilesson on working well with a partner, students disperse around the room to work with partners on a piece of writing. Moving around the room, Colleen and Deana use their phones to snap photos of pairs of writers at work. They quickly upload the photos to a computer attached to the room's projector. Then, back on the rug after writing, students look at the photos (see Figures 2.5 and 2.6) and talk about what they remember doing.

First, we ask the writers pictured to narrate for their classmates what they are doing in the photo. We find that, aided by the photo, our students can more clearly recall what is happening. Where previously they might have debriefed partner work by saying, "I talked with my partner about my writing," or "My partner helped me with my writing," the photos seem to help them access specific actions and events:

"I'm explaining what I want to write next."

"I'm listening to Robbie tell about how he wants to end the story."

"We are looking at Leticia's house map in her notebook so she can choose something to write about next."

"I'm helping Leticia label her map with another story place."

Figure 2.5   Partners at Work

Figure 2.6   Partners at Work

Next, the whole group reflects on these firsthand rememberings elicited by the photos. All the writers in the room can connect their own partner experiences to those of the students pictured; kids jump in to share how they did something similar or different. Teachers, too, reflect on what we see in the photos that we want students to notice: "I'm struck by how the writers are making eye contact. It signals to me that they are really listening to one another."

Unpacking Photo Elicitation

When you learn to do something new, whether it's knitting, cooking, dancing, raising a baby, or tending a garden, don't you sometimes long just to compare notes with someone else? Just to *see* how they go about it? You can confirm your own sense of things, learn from another person's successes and mistakes, or find out that your way is not the only way—either to try what someone else is doing or to feel more sure about what *you* are doing. It's the same with our student writers. Photo elicitation helps us remember with depth and detail the experiences of brave writers so we can learn from them in powerful ways.

The talk that comes from photo elicitation is a lot like that bonus voice-over track on a DVD where the director talks about what went on behind the scenes as the film is playing. But our second and third graders haven't seen much director commentary, so we find it helpful to prompt them with questions that start simply but can progress as they get more experience:

- What do you see in the photo?
- What is happening in this moment?
- What happened before this moment? What happened after this moment?
- Why is this happening?
- What else could you have done then? And why did you elect not to do it?
- What's left out of the picture that you think we should know about?

Questions like these prompt students to really *look* at the photos and just describe them first. We hope this helps break whatever assumptions students might have about their processes or about what we think their processes *should* be—better to simply notice and learn from what they have *actually* done. Prompted to look closely at the photos and describe what they see, students might notice things they hadn't been aware of when the photos were taken. The more complex questions help student writers place what they're seeing in context, think about what happened connected to a particular moment, and link specific images of work in progress to their sense of how and why they were doing what they did.

In the snapshot of this strategy, teachers took the photos, but students can also learn a lot from taking photos *themselves*. Just deciding what to picture in the photo provokes important questions: Where can I put the camera that would best show

invitation *to* REFLECT

Have a colleague or any adult pop into your class for a few minutes to take some photos of writing workshop (or take some yourself). Do the same for your colleague. Then, meet and talk about what you notice. The photos will help you remember what happened and prompt you as you describe that to your colleague.

what I am doing as a writer? What moves, what artifacts, what faces, or what words do I need in the frame to capture this decision or moment? In other words, when choosing what to record and how, students are already engaged in a kind of remembering—that is, actively shaping the form of the memories they will have to draw upon. We value this activity as practice in the deliberate manipulation of their own attention. That is, remembering isn't just thinking back and retrieving what you can. Remembering fully involves deciding, when doing something, that it might be worth remembering at all. It means knowing even while writing that "this is something I may want to think more about later." When students place the camera and snap a photo, they are deliberately choosing to remember.

Video, of course, can also be used for photo elicitation. Teachers or students can record each other, cameras can be mounted on tripods, or individual students can wear a GoPro camera while they're working. A single writer might use video to do some private reflecting, but we think video is even more valuable when the whole class looks closely at one writer's process. Just as you might confer with one student in front of the whole class as a teaching strategy—going deep into one case as an example for others—you can play the video and pause to have the student explain what he or she was doing in the footage. Then you can ask questions to draw out the what, how, and why of the student's decision making.

invitation *to* REFLECT

Here are some more ideas about how you might use remembering for your own reflection as a teacher. Think of a teaching incident that you want to better understand. Maybe it's a troublesome interaction with a student or a lesson that didn't work as well as you hoped. Write about it using these prompts:

- ◆ Jot or sketch a list or storyboard of key events in the incident.
- ◆ List sensory details and words you recall from the incident.
- ◆ Describe the context—what else was going on at the time of the incident?
- ◆ From what perspective are you remembering? If you take someone else's role for a moment, can you remember anything different?
- ◆ What was important to you at the time?

chapter

THREE
THREE

Writers Describe

For about twenty years, our friend Jessica has done yoga almost every day. She attends yoga retreats, reads about yoga, and considers the practice of yoga an important part of who she is. We (Colleen, Deana, and Anne) also have done yoga, but with nothing like that frequency or dedication. Jessica is a yogi; we are three women who have been to yoga classes once in a while! If the three of us talk about doing yoga, we might use words such as these:

easy	flexible
relaxing	difficult
Downward Dog	stretch my legs
hip joints	

But when Jessica talks about yoga, her words are more like this:

asanas	Adho Mukha Svanasana
IT band	holding tension
deepen the pose	

In other words, Jessica has learned specific language for aspects of yoga that matter. They are terms from Sanskrit, from human anatomy, and from the community of fellow yoga practitioners who are next to her on their mats each day and with whom she talks regularly about yoga after class. We can say, "Wow, when I was doing Downward Dog, it really stretched my legs; that felt great." Jessica can say, "In Adho Mukha Svanasana today, I was able to really deepen the pose by focusing on relaxing my hamstrings and feeling my weight evenly spread across my hands and feet. Last week I had a lot more tension in that pose." Jessica can talk about yoga at length and in detail. She has words that distinguish between different episodes in her experience and different outcomes in each episode. We're all thinking back, and thinking usefully, about what we have done, but Jessica has a much greater repertoire of language to use to talk about her experience. And her language can connect her to others in the yoga community as well as help her realize things that would make her practice even more meaningful and help her grow.

Similarly, having specific, shared language to talk about writing is important for writers to reflect with others in the classroom community. Consider Hye-Su's response when Deana asked her which of the three leads she'd written for her narrative was her favorite. Hye-Su said, "I really like the original one where I started with a character talking. But I tried these other two: one with action happening right away and one with a description of the setting. After I tried those, I picked my original; I like it best and she really is the main character. My partner reader liked it too!"

Hye-Su was able to use writing-specific words such as *leads*, *character*, *description*, and *setting* to talk about her work. And she could describe how and why she made decisions: "I tried . . . ," "I picked . . . ," "My partner reader . . ." She was fluent in describing her work as a writer. This helped her learn from the experience *and* connected her to our learning as a class.

Students grow into the language of writers over time. In August, a student might complete the sentence "I'm a writer who likes to write . . . " with the single word *stories*, and that's a great start. We are happy if she already likes to write stories when she comes to us! But by June, we expect a richer answer, something more like this: "I really enjoy writing realistic fiction, because I can draw on things in my real life. But fantasy can be fun too!" The student has more to say, and that alone is valuable, but when we notice her language, we get even more excited. She can name different kinds of stories—realistic fiction and fantasy—and she also has experienced writing these genres enough to have a preference between them. Because she can name her preferences, she can connect with other writers in the class who also love these same kinds of writing. *And* her language points specifically to a process for generating ideas in a certain genre: in realistic fiction, she can draw on her own life. This writer can effectively describe when she reflects on her experiences with writing.

Writers also learn to describe the process of writing. Consider the language in this comment:

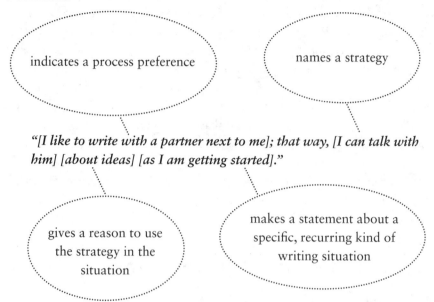

This writer knows writing—and his own process as a writer—well enough to name it in specific terms: when *this* happens, and I need *this*, I can do *this*.

If students don't have the language to describe themselves and their actions as writers, they can give their impressions of an experience, but it's difficult to get specific enough to make those impressions very useful. In other words, *language matters*.

Specific Language Signals Membership in a Community

Imagine two friends at a Super Bowl party. One is a hard-core football fan who watches regularly; the other is there mostly for the commercials. As the game unfolds, one friend uses terms like *down*, *holding*, *wildcat offense*, and *audible*. The other partygoers know that she likes and understands football; they pick up on these cues and engage her in a lively discussion about the game. The other friend overhears these conversations, and she understands them to a point, but she can't really jump in. It's the same way with student writers. Knowing and using our in-group terms signal membership in our writing workshop. Students belong to our literacy club (Smith 1988), with all the rights and privileges of membership.

What's more, when students have domain-specific language for describing writing and writing processes, they can converse with writers anywhere. They can connect to writers across different levels and different circumstances. For instance, Anne's own two children are in kindergarten and fifth grade. Obviously, they are at very different levels of learning in writing: five-year-old William is working on things like end punctuation, having stories of more than one or two sentences, and adding detail to the drawings that constitute a big part of his writing. Emily is working on things like citing evidence when making a claim and constructing multiclause sentences correctly. Yet both of these young writers can talk about shared experiences with writing processes: they can say, "I felt stuck," or "I used a bubble cluster to get ideas"; they can say, "I revised to make my writing more clear," or "I am almost ready to publish." Having language for what we do as writers links us to other writers. Students with this rich capacity for describing their work as writers can walk into a different classroom and have a basis for entering the discussion in that community.

Specific Language Makes It Possible to Give and Receive Feedback

Maybe you've had this experience: In a college course, you were so confused you didn't even know what you were confused about. You would have gone to the professor's office hours, but what question would you even have asked? Or maybe you've taken a sick child to the doctor and found it's hard to know how to help if a child can't articulate anything more specific than "It hurts." Well, the writing version of "It hurts" is often "I'm stuck," and if students can't say much beyond that, it can be hard to know how to help them.

The ability to describe experiences is the key to sharing them with other people, but our students begin the year unable to say much about what they do as writers other than "I write." How, then, can they talk in detail about their process and decision making? To reflect on something together, writers need to put their partners *inside* a memory so they can inhabit it together, take a look around, and compare experiences. We want students to have language to describe writing when it is great but also when it gets hard, as it so often does, and they need words to recount writing strategies they have tried so they can give or receive feedback. Students need words like these:

- ◆ "I like experimenting with different leads depending on the audience I choose for my writing."

- ◆ "I need quiet time when I am getting started, but later on I like partner writing so I can ask questions when I need someone."

- ◆ "My first topic was problematic for me. The topic I have now is more productive."

When students can clearly describe their situations, needs, and experiences as writers, they can better seek and receive help with their writing. This can be extremely powerful when conferring with writers. When students are empowered to describe what they need to grow as writers, it makes conferring time more meaningful and tailored to the needs of individual students.

Teaching Writers to Describe

One of our students, Tanya, is working on a fractured fairy tale, a revision of the story of Cinderella she has titled "Ela". Her story has many, many female characters, and originally it was difficult for a reader to keep track of them. What's more, the many characters were indistinguishable from one another. For example, if all the stepsisters are now nice and also have no names or other identifying characteristics, how is a reader to follow along? It wasn't clear. Now that she has addressed these issues, Tanya gives us an account of her work on this story:

"I was reading to my partner, and she was getting confused in my story. It was kind of all over the place. I put these little stars [*pointing*] in places that needed more. Then I added detail. I wrote the new parts to add over here on the other page [the facing page in her notebook]. Like here, I added how the first sister was a great dancer. I revised to put in all the things I needed to make the story more complete. I included dialogue so that the sisters would come to life and be more real. Also, parts of it I had started but sort of forgot about; I ended up taking out some of the people who didn't turn into full characters. I like it a lot better this way because I think it's more of a story now."

Tanya sounds like a kid, not a professional writer, but she sounds like a kid who has given her work some thought and has learned some things from her experience. Her description focuses less on the text itself and more on the actions she has taken in shaping it. Her words show us she's remembering the three aspects of her experience we highlighted in the last chapter, and she has language to describe each one: *what* she did as a writer (adding details, adding dialogue, deleting characters), *how* she did it (using stars and the facing page), and *why* she did it (to be less confusing to the reader and bring characters to life).

In Chapter 2, we shared a few of the tools we use to help students remember their writing experiences. In this chapter we share some explicit lessons we teach to help students develop rich writing metalanguage for describing *what*, *how*, and *why*—the kind of language Tanya is using here. We should note that we don't actually separate the metalanguage into these categories in practice; we simply teach our students to describe what they do as writers. But recognizing these different ways writers describe their experiences helps us teach with more intention. So first, let's briefly consider each type of language separately.

DESCRIBING *WHAT*

First, we want students to be able to describe the *what* of their writing experiences. What happened? What situation arose? What did you try? What did you do? What was the outcome of that action? In other words, what was the context or problem, and what was the solution or failed solution?

Tanya describes *what* when she says, "[My partner] was getting confused in my story. It was kind of all over the place." She's identifying a problem and naming it. She also describes *what* when she mentions particular details of her text: "stars," "new parts," "characters," and "dialogue." She has language to describe both her text and the situation she faces with it.

We know students are getting better at describing *what* when they use nouns to name kinds of writing or parts of a text or use adjectives that describe problems or aspects of a text, like the ones listed in Figure 3.1.

When writers describe *what*, they name and give specific details about what they are trying to accomplish in a text or with a writing practice.

Guiding Questions for Describing *What*

- ◆ Can you name the following?
  - ◆ what you are trying to do
  - ◆ different problems you had
  - ◆ different strategies you used or thought of using but decided not to
- ◆ [In response to something a student tries to describe] Is there a term for this? On our word wall or elsewhere in this classroom, do we have any words that would help you describe this?

◆ Can you break what you just said about your writing process into steps? Can you name the different things that go into what you just said?

◆ How could you describe that to someone who wasn't here today?

Nouns	Adjectives
(naming aspects of texts, text types, or text parts; naming classroom resources)	(characterizing a text or problem in a text; often modifying nouns listed to the left)
narrative	jumbled, all over the place
fantasy	exciting
table of contents	organized
lead	complicated
climax	incomplete
characters	convincing
dialogue	helpful
paragraphs	difficult
partner	vivid
conference	flowing
word wall	realistic
ideas	
storyteller voice	

Figure 3.1 Examples of Specific Language for Describing *What*

DESCRIBING *HOW*

Our students also need specific language to describe *how* they do things, to narrate processes they use to solve the problems they encounter in writing. And when they write well, we want them to explain how they did it, both to share their new expertise with peers and so they can remember what to do in similar situations. When writers describe *how*, they identify and name specific steps they took along the way in a given writing experience.

When Tanya talks about the changes she made in "Ela," we hear a writer who knows how to use specific words to describe her process and the actions she decided to take. For example, Tanya says she "*was reading* to [her] partner," "*put* these little stars," "*added* detail" and "*revised*." She uses writing-specific verbs to tell her writing story in first person, detailing the actions she took to address the problems she noticed in her text. Because they name actions, writers use writing-specific verbs to describe *how* (see Figure 3.2).

Guiding Questions for Describing *How*

- ◆ I noticed that you did _____; how did you do that?
- ◆ How did you share that with your readers?
- ◆ How did you think about your writing?
- ◆ How did this come to be?
- ◆ How could another writer do what you have done here with this beginning?

Verbs That Describe Thinking and Action	Verbs That Describe Changes to the Writing Itself
thought	added
noticed	revised
wondered	changed
considered	reorganized
experimented	moved
selected	deleted
discovered	

Figure 3.2   Examples of Specific Language for Describing **How**

DESCRIBING *WHY*

Finally, to learn from an experience in writing, students have to do more than just describe what they did and how they did it: they also need to consider *why* they made certain decisions as writers.

Tanya actually begins with *why* in her reflection when she describes her partner's confused reaction to her story. All the actions she took were grounded in the needs of her reader, and she is very specific about the rationale for each revision she made:

- ◆ "I revised to put in all the things I needed to make the story more complete."

- ◆ "I included dialogue so that the sisters would come to life and be more real."

- ◆ "I ended up taking out some of the people who didn't turn into full characters."

In describing the *why* of her experience, Tanya names and narrates her decision making. Figure 3.3 offers a few examples of the kinds of terms we hear our student writers using when they describe *why*.

Words That Signal a Writer Might Be Describing *Why*	Words That Name Reasons for Decisions
because	to clarify
so	to explain
so that	to improve
in order to	my reader needed
	I wanted to communicate
	my audience would/wouldn't

Figure 3.3   Examples of Specific Language for Describing *Why*

Language that describes *why* explains—and sometimes justifies—a writer's choices and decisions.

Guiding Questions for Describing *Why*

- ◆ What led to that choice?

- ◆ I saw you chose to ____; what else did you consider? (We realize this question actually asks *what*, but we find students answer with a *why*.)

- ◆ What difference did that make?

invitation *to* REFLECT

How might you enrich your own vocabulary for describing writing experiences? One great way is to read writers' work on writing. Notice how these writers describe their craft and the terms they use. Some of our favorites:

- *On Writing: A Memoir of the Craft*, by Stephen King (New York: Scribner, 2000)

- *Bird by Bird: Some Instructions on Writing and Life*, by Anne Lamott (New York: Anchor, 1995)

- *Countdown to "Breakout"* (www.katemessner.com/category/countdowntobreakout/), by Kate Messner. This set of blog posts takes you (and students) through the entire process of writing and publishing Messner's young readers' novel *Breakout*, with up-close looks at how and why she makes decisions along the way.

When writers reflect, they describe *what*, *how*, and *why* simultaneously. Yet we hope you can see how describing *why* is really at the heart of it all because it speaks to students' agency and decision making. When we ask students to describe why they've done things as writers, we communicate an important message: that they can and must make decisions as they are writing and that "because the teacher asked me to do it this way" is not a sufficient reason for doing anything. Our students will eventually move forward as writers—to other classrooms and the world—without us, so they have to own their decision making. We value describing *why* for all the same reasons we value choice in any writing classroom—not just because it is fun (though it is fun) but because our students learn to write when they are free to make choices and find out what happens as a result.

Strategies for Describing

In our classrooms each day, we are careful to use writing-specific language in all our teaching and our interactions with student writers. Over time, we've also developed strategies to help students learn and use this specific language to reflect on their work in writing workshop. We share four of those strategies here: (1) making a "Verbs Writers Do" chart; (2) adding writing process terms to the word wall; (3) sorting process and product statements; and (4) conducting process interviews.

"VERBS WRITERS DO" CHART

Writing is made up of so many concurrent and interrelated processes, it boggles the mind. Even when writing a simple grocery list, you have to remember things you have recently run out of, visualize what is (and isn't) in your fridge, decide what you want to have for dinner in the coming week, identify ingredients for those meals, compare the ingredients you need with what you have on hand, select words to write down for each item on the list (Is "milk" enough, or do you need to specify "skim milk"? It might depend on who is going to the store.), spell those words correctly (or at least correctly enough to read), file the list somewhere it can be retrieved . . . it's a lot! And that's just for a list where you're the only audience; things get even more complicated for students who are working in specific genres, for specific audiences, with specific content, and with developing writing skills—including handwriting, new vocabulary, and conventions of standard written English. So, when writers write, they don't *just* write; they remember, visualize, decide, select, spell, and more.

One way we help our students understand the complexity of writing is by working on a chart we call "Verbs Writers Do." We start by asking the class at the beginning of a writing lesson: "What are some of the things you do when you write?" As the class brainstorms, we chart, and we typically get a list that looks something like the one in Figure 3.4.

After we make this initial list, we ask children, "When you go off to write today, can you try to notice all you are doing as you work? We're going to see if we can add to this list." And off they go, to work on whatever they've been working on, alone or in pairs, spread out across the room. As they work, we move around the room,

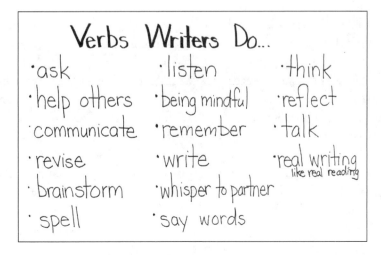

Figure 3.4 An Initial List of Verbs Writers Do

conferring. And as we confer, we try to use specific verbs to describe to students what we see them doing.

"What are you working on?"

"I'm doing the story I started yesterday about my dog."

"Oh, so you're continuing to *draft* that!"

These interactions are short and simple; mostly we want the students to be writing, and we don't want to interrupt that flow too much.

At the end of writing time, we meet back at the carpet and we make a teaching decision. If it's early in the year, or if the initial list of verbs is thin, we usually decide to have students simply add to the list. We know that after writing for a while, they will almost always realize they are taking actions they hadn't thought to include at first—actions such as thinking and decision making. Often, students realize they talk a lot during working time, which leads us to questions. How do we categorize talk? Is that part of writing? When in writing did we talk? What did it help us to do? A line of questioning like this can help us build a case for the power of productive talk. In essence, our first objective with the "Verbs Writers Do" chart is simply to help students notice that they actually *do* a lot when they write!

Later in the year, or if the initial list of actions writers take is really robust, we can extend students' thinking by helping them dig deeper into the significance of those actions. While writers are working, we take a pair of scissors to the chart, cutting it apart so each verb is on its own strip of paper. On a new chart, we make categories: "Before Writing," "While Writing," "After Writing," and "Always" or "Throughout." As a group, we go through the verbs we generated earlier, and we attach each one in the appropriate category on the chart. This leads to a lot of rich conversation about when various actions occur. For example, if the verb is "thinking," do we think before writing? While writing? Throughout? One student will say "talk with partner" is something she does after writing, to see places to improve, and another will say she does it before writing, to get ideas. One student will name "spelling" as something she does while writing, spelling each word as she needs it, and another will share that he just spells it the best he can while writing, but really thinks about spelling more carefully *after* writing, when it won't slow him down. The categories break down right away—but it's the *way* they break down that is so instructive. (See Figure 3.5.)

The "Verbs Writers Do" chart is not meant to be one total word bank of all writing terms. We do generate a mighty list of words, but our aim now is more about students' attention to processes in progress. The list helps students understand

Figure 3.5   Chart of Verbs Arranged by Categories

that the verb *write* is layered and complex and that more precise terms are called for if we're going to talk about writing with much success. We're building students' ability to mindfully engage in doing while also observing themselves doing—noticing actions they take and naming those actions.

Students benefit most from this strategy when they generate the word list themselves, reaching for the terms that describe their own activities as they remember them. That doesn't mean, however, that you shouldn't also be introducing students to new words naturally through conversation—in conferences, minilessons, and share times—to spice up the pot of terms they can use to describe their work as writers. Figure 3.6 is a word bank of precise verbs you might use as you talk with students about writing.

invent	reflect	embellish
create	notice	improve
write	seek help	grow
draft	help	develop
think	partner	illustrate
wonder	check	edit
list	revise	correct
jot	rearrange	refine
do a brain dump	(re)organize	proofread
consider	delete	publish
think	add	share
reread	elaborate	get/give feedback
		polish

Figure 3.6   Verbs That Describe Writers' Actions

WRITING PROCESS WORD WALL

Another way to develop language for describing writing experiences is to teach students writing terms just as you would teach any other important vocabulary. Like many teachers, we have a word wall routine where students and teachers suggest interesting new words, write them on sentence strips, briefly define them, and then hang them on the classroom cabinets alphabetically. Students use the word wall as a resource to remember a word's meaning or spelling.

The "Verbs Writers Do" chart and the word wall can easily work hand in hand. Many of the verbs on the chart are process terms, such as *prewrite*, *revise*, and *edit*. As these terms come up, we add them to the wall. There's no great ceremony about it; after using a term with the class for the first time, we just say, "This is an important word. I'm going to add it to the word wall." Later in the year, students can add writing terms to the word wall on their own, though we do encourage clear, legible handwriting since the wall is a resource for all writers, including English language learners, many of whom are transitioning to our alphabet.

As the wall begins to fill with writing-specific vocabulary, when we hear a term or use a term, we point to the word on the wall (or add it if it's not already there). "Remember what I mean when I say *editing*? See, it's up on the word wall." We take care to notice when writing-specific terms might be useful, use them ourselves, and then explicitly teach them. This happens organically more than strategically, but we do try to be mindful of two important times for referring kids to the word wall: in conferring and in whole-group reflection time after writing. As students talk about their work as writers in either of these settings, we simply name what they are doing using target language from the wall (see Figure 3.7).

When students say things like . . .	We say things like . . .
I'm rearranging these different parts of my piece.	Oh, you're *revising*! Oh, you're *reorganizing*! That will make your writing more *coherent*!
She fixed my writing for me.	Was her *feedback* useful? She's helping you *edit*? Did she *proofread* your writing for you? How did she help you to *revise*?
I don't know what to do next.	Hmm, what will your *audience* be wondering now? What *revision* might make sense for you?

Figure 3.7 Conferring with Writing Terms from the Word Wall

When we direct students' attention to a word on the wall, we make it explicit, often directing a student to go and point to the word we are using. Our own adult eyes scan quickly to find a word we already can picture in our heads, but for students, it's not so easy. We want to locate that resource in the students' mental map of the room so they can go right to it, not read every single word around the room as they search.

Figure 3.8   Word Wall Examples

We can't stress enough how important we think this work is, even though we know it's a simple, common teaching practice. We all also teach adults—all three of us work with teacher candidates at the university, and Anne also has master's and doctoral students. These very intelligent, very accomplished adults also struggle to articulate their needs and their processes as writers. Just like our elementary school students, they often talk about "fixing" their writing when they might mean anything from invention, to organizing ideas, to revising, to learning from feedback, to editing, to proofreading. And they, too, find they can seek and receive writing help more effectively when they have words to explain what they're doing and what they've tried.

PROCESS AND PRODUCT STATEMENT SORTING

Another way we teach students to describe their work as writers is to help them distinguish between product and process. In a Google document, we record a number of statements students make about writing—things we jot down while they are working and we are conferring. Sometimes, we confess, we also write down things we *wish* writers had said (things they *might* have said but didn't necessarily say that day). We typically end up with a list like this:

- "I looked in my notebook for ideas for a new piece of writing."
- "I'm writing about when my dog died."
- "My narrative needs a more exciting beginning."
- "I tried two different leads."
- "My partner helped me think of a way to change my story."
- "I added dialogue."
- "My table of contents includes seven chapters."
- "I'm deciding between a map here or a picture of the main character."
- "I had trouble getting all these ideas to fit together."

Near the end of writing time, we enlarge the font on the document to 18 points or more, hit Print, and grab the paper from the printer. Then, using a simple T-chart on the easel with columns labeled "Product" and "Process," we work as a class to sort the statements into the two categories. Scissors in hand, we snip a statement off the list and pose the question to our students—usually in more than one way—as we consider each statement:

- "Does this tell about the thing she is writing, or does it tell about how she is writing it?"
- "Does it give us an idea what his story is like, or does it help us see how he is making the story that way?"
- "Is this sentence about something your writing is doing or something you are doing?"

Many times, the key to categorizing the statements is noticing the subject and the verb. If the subject is the writer, then it's most likely a process statement. For example, in "I tried two different leads," *tried* is the verb, and *I* (the writer) is the subject. If the subject is some part of the text, as in "My table of contents includes seven chapters" or "My narrative needs a more exciting beginning," then the statement is almost always about the product.

Sometimes students disagree about which column a statement belongs in, and this always leads to thoughtful discussion, so we often invite students to agree or disagree with a statement's placement. For example, when we were considering the statement "I tried two different leads," a student said it described process because "I tried" gave an account of steps the writer took in the process of composing the text. Certainly the subject-and-verb rule suggested it should be classified as a process statement, but we still wanted to invite thinking. So we placed the statement in the "Process" column, but then we asked students to indicate with a hand gesture whether they agreed with the placement or not. When a student disagreed, we asked him to explain. He noted that of the two leads this writer tried, one ended up in the final piece of writing. So, this student argued, it was a statement about a product.

Of course, some statements do include both process and product. For example, one fifth grader told Anne, "I want a diagram here so I can show how women's gymnastics has four events and men's has six, but I don't know how to draw it." In a way, this is a statement about the finished product, which will include a diagram. But in another way, this is a statement about process: I am having trouble making the writing do what I want.

Figuring out precisely where a statement fits can be quite challenging, but precision itself is not really that important. The value of the activity is in *thinking* about where a statement fits, not in knowing for sure. The more we make distinctions between processes and products, the less likely our students are to conflate them. And this matters to us, because ultimately it's students' experiences with writing *processes* that are cumulative and instructive, even as particular products are completed and fall from memory.

Understanding the difference between process and product also helps students distinguish between the writer and the text. We want students to know, "My writing is not me. I can feel pride that I tried several strategies in a writing session, even when my text still needs a lot of work." Students need to be able to differentiate between actions and outcomes. Of course these are linked—if a student can say, "I spent time getting feedback from a partner," she will probably also someday be able to say her finished product is stronger as a result. But not always, and rarely right away! Sometimes it takes time for the processes we engage in to have visible effects on our finished writing. That doesn't mean those processes aren't worthwhile.

Making a distinction between process and product is also very helpful in goal setting. Our writers set goals for themselves at multiple points throughout the year, and when they do, they set one or more product goals (outcomes they would like to see in the writing they produce) as well as one or more process goals (actions they would like to take as writers). A student who sets a product goal to "write longer pieces," for example, will need to think about the actions she will take to accomplish this goal. What will she have to do to produce longer texts? Well, she might choose a better place to sit during writing time so she can get more done in class. Or she might add an elaboration step to her drafting process that will help her add more detail. Distinguishing between writing processes and written products helps students claim agency over process and work with intention to affect the outcome of a written product. We say more about goal setting in Chapter 5.

PROCESS INTERVIEWS

Once the year is underway and students have experience in making different decisions as writers, they can gain valuable practice through describing their work in process interviews with peers. Students form pairs and bring their notebooks and drafts to a quiet place to talk as partners. "Be like a detective," we tell them. "Try to find out every single detail you can about your partner's writing process. Solve this mystery: *How* did he or she make this piece of writing?"

Figure 3.9 shows some of the questions we offer students to support their detective work. Note that we do not simply hand this list out. It's too long; many of our younger students couldn't read this much text, or the handout itself would take over and remove students' own questions from the center of the work. Instead, we share one or two of these questions as starters and then ask students to add a few of their own before we turn them loose to work. We move around as students are interviewing each other, and if we find a pair whose well of questions seems to have run dry, we offer a new question to help them get back on track.

- What was the very first thing you did to start this piece of writing? (Then what? Then what?)

- What was a problem you had along the way? (What other problems came up? Were there problems after that?)

- How did you know you needed to do this?

- Is this something you have done in some other piece of writing before? How did you know to try it again?

- What led to that choice?

- What were the steps involved in doing that?

- Where did you get that idea?

- What other ways of doing it did you consider?

- What did you try before that? After that?

- What did you try that *didn't* work?

- What did you do along the way that you really want to remember for next time?

Figure 3.9 Questions for Process Interviews

invitation *to* REFLECT

Try the questions in Figure 3.9 for yourself. Meet with a teacher-writer colleague and interview each other. Or, you can even interview yourself into a voice recorder and then play back your responses and see what you can notice.

After students have had ample time to interview, we bring them back together for whole-group reflection. We ask, "Who can tell us about a partner who did something interesting or helpful?" and then students report out. While the goal of process interviews is for writers to narrate their decision making in their own words, we find that having partners narrate in this way is also helpful. Sometimes a partner uses more vivid or specific words than the writer initially used in the interview. Other times, the one reporting out is at a loss for words, and we turn to the writer and say, "Can you help her out?"

As students share, we ask follow-up questions to help them move from describing actions ("I added some details.") to describing *decisions* ("My partner was confused about who was who in my story. So, I added some details to make the characters more real and more different from each other.") The second description has more words, and those words more clearly describe the writer's actions, but the writer is also owning the decision in an important way—she added detail because she saw a need, not because her teacher said to add detail. This level of detail in reflection helps writers turn experiences, and our teaching, into their own learning.

We generally just turn pairs of kids loose to interview each other, but you might consider offering students more support when you start. For example, you might conduct a process interview with another teacher in front of your students, letting them hear how you describe your choices as writers. Similarly, you might interview a student writer in front of students and then step back and point to specific descriptive words the student used that helped you understand his process. Or a student might interview you. Once students are familiar with interviewing, it's also possible to have them self-interview on a video app such as Seesaw, which can then be shared with the classroom community—including parents (this reminds us of the confessional booth on TV shows like *The Real World* and *Survivor*!).

invitation *to* REFLECT

Just as your students can better reflect when
describing writing, here are some more prompts
reflect on your teaching. After doing a quickwri
your teaching, ask yourself:

- ◆ What is this story really about?
- ◆ What is this a case of?
- ◆ What terms or language of my professional community apply here?
- ◆ What questions can be asked about this story?
- ◆ What other situations is it similar to or in contrast to? (Read back in your notebook.)
- ◆ How does this story not fit with what I know or believe?
- ◆ What does it make me feel now?
- ◆ What does it make me wonder now?

chapter

FOUR

Writers Act

What's the point of remembering writing experiences clearly, or of having language to describe and analyze those experiences, if it doesn't lead a writer to act more strategically next time? The third component of scaffolding reflection helps students *act* upon the insights they have gained through reflection, set specific intentions, and develop a habit of invoking those intentions the next time they write. We see this step as imperative, given our commitment to "teaching the writer, not the writing" (Calkins 1994, 228). Any one piece of writing will soon be either finished or abandoned, but the writer—through subsequent action—will keep going.

Action is really the whole point of reflection, but too often students are asked to "do reflection," which is a nice way to think about things, but it doesn't go anywhere. For example, in Anne's early days as a high school teacher, she often reserved the day an assignment was due for reflective writing. After completing a major writing task such as an essay, students would spend time in class writing a process piece, narrating the process by which they had written and revised the paper. At the end of the period, students stapled their reflections to their essays and dropped them in Anne's inbox for her long weekend of grading. The students' reflections helped Anne know what to focus on as she read their work and they were invaluable to her planning, so they weren't completely useless, but what did they do for her *students*? Anne's students turned their reflections in, usually on a Friday, and the next Monday they were starting something new, without those reflections in hand or in mind.

We want to do better than this with our elementary writers. We want them to be able to draw on their past experiences with intention, and we know it's not enough to simply hope that what they've learned will stick. Peter Brown, Henry Roediger, and Mark McDaniel show in their book *Make It Stick* (2014) that for learning to be retrievable later, you not only must acquire the knowledge and file it somewhere but also need to practice actually retrieving it. That is, it's not enough to learn something; you also need to learn how to *call upon* that learning when you need it. Focusing on action within reflection responds to this need.

Action Helps Writers Move Forward

Hannah is a third grader who is writing an informational piece all about bearded dragons. She is an expert on the topic because she has one as a pet and has also researched them at home and at school. As she reads over her chapter drafts and her table of contents, she becomes pensive when talking to Deana. "I'm worried I have too many chapters. The last time I had too many chapters, I didn't have enough information to add to each of them."

Sitting with her notebook on the floor in front of them both, Deana asks, "Do you have an idea of how you want to change your table of contents? Because it does appear that you have a lot of important information to share."

Hannah ponders the question for a moment and then makes a decision: "I think I will combine my chapters about heat and light with 'How to Care for Your Pet.' I may also combine 'What Do They Look Like?' with 'Camouflage.' That way, I will still have all of the information in my book but will be able to get rid of two chapters that I didn't have enough information to write about." Hannah was reflecting on her work before Deana even sat down with her. Connecting her present situation with past writing experiences, she is now able to set intentions and then act on her ideas by changing the organization of her book.

Hannah's ability to do this reveals socioemotional learning on her part, developed and deployed in concert with her expertise as a writer (Taylor et al. 2017). That is, Hannah not only knows how to read the writing situation and what it calls for but also knows how to manage her own feelings about writing, even on the days when it doesn't sound fun or when the going gets tough. She knows how to plan for projects that extend across multiple days and to remember what she has been doing across that span of time so she can get back into her work after time away. And she knows enough about her own working environment, and her personal propensities for distraction or efficiency in that environment, to plan to get her work done.

So many of us are not quite as efficient as Hannah. We mean to do something next time, but when that time rolls around we don't do it. We forget that the Thanksgiving stuffing tasted better with less sage, or that the snowman math lesson worked better if the marshmallows were already counted out, until we're in the thick of a familiar situation and realize we failed to act on what we thought we had learned the year before. If action is so important, why is it so hard to act? We see a couple of barriers to action, time and patterns, both of which are worth considering if we are to help students take action.

THE PROBLEM OF TIME

Time can be the enemy of action. Often, a lot of time passes between when a student learns something from an experience and when he faces a similar situation and needs to draw on that learning. Math, science, social studies, reading, music, lunch, recess, family time: all of these occur between one writing workshop and the next, every single day. For children who are still learning the clock and the calendar, and whose time lines for daily living are largely determined by others, those stretches of time between writing periods can be very, very long. Weekends are long. Vacations are long. After a few days away—say, a snow delay, some district testing, or perhaps a school assembly—many children have forgotten what they were doing. It takes some deliberate effort to revive the flow of working on a piece of writing.

What's more, children write slowly compared with adults, and their work is mostly completed in very short segments over long stretches of time. For example, as we composed this book, we might have written a paragraph in a few minutes, or a page or so in an hour, with some paragraphs and some pages taking much longer when we were struggling to work out an idea. But our second- and third-grade students produce writing more slowly. They're most often writing by hand. Many are still thinking about forming each letter. Most are inventing the spelling for half their words. A significant proportion of our writers are also learning English, arriving in the United States even in midyear. Each word and sentence takes time. And they're also learning how to make themselves work, how to make good decisions about whom to sit with, and how to contend with distractions. So, what our students accomplish in twenty to forty minutes of writing time is a significant accomplishment, but it's usually *not* that much text. Thus they contend with an often interrupted process when it comes to constructing a longer text, revising a piece of writing over time. This can make drawing on past experiences to take new action more of a challenge.

THE PROBLEM OF PATTERNS

Not only does time make taking action on reflection difficult but so does the problem of patterns. To better understand how patterns make it hard to act, it helps to draw on adult experiences. Take dating, for example. How many of us have started up a new relationship and felt everything was going well, only to realize that our new partner was a lot like a previous partner or our own behavior was very like our behavior in a previous relationship? We all form patterns of behavior, and once formed, these patterns are hard to break, especially when we travel a ways down the road before we realize we are stuck—again—in the familiar pattern. And even though the pattern may seem obvious in retrospect, in the flow of experience, we fail to recognize signs that we've been there before.

It's the same with our student writers. For example, take Maryam, a second grader. At the beginning of the year, writing narratives, Maryam tended to lose track of her story. What started as a princess walking in a forest suddenly became a group of dogs talking to one another, and she seemed to forget the princess altogether. Later, when writing an informational book on Dubai (where she had spent time with family), Maryam composed a set of single sentences related to Dubai, but she rarely connected one to another. One sentence might describe a delicious food and another name a pool she visited; she seemed to forget that she had planned to address food, activities, and other topics in separate chapters. As her teachers, we saw these problems as part of a larger pattern in which Maryam struggled to organize her thoughts. But did she see it?

Ideally, we'd like a student like Maryam to have "organization" as a category in her head and be able to recognize many types of writing situations as being *about* organization—structuring a narrative, keeping sentences on different aspects of a topic grouped with one another, and planning a table of contents and referring back to it while writing. Writers who recognize their own patterns have a much better chance of taking positive action to address them each time they set out to write.

Strategies for Acting

Three strategies we use with students to help them take action are (1) connective sentence stems, (2) sticky note planning, and (3) accountability partners. These take us from a vague *hope* that our students will apply lessons they have learned in writing workshop to actually *supporting* them in doing so.

CONNECTIVE SENTENCE STEMS

One strategy we have come to value to help students act with intention is to simply ask them to articulate what learning or insight they plan to carry forward. At the end of a writing experience (usually when students have completed a finished piece of writing), we use a sentence stem to structure this kind of thinking. We know how important classroom language is in supporting students' thinking and their acquisition of the discourses of academic and civic life (Johnston 2004). Sentence frames are certainly nothing new—many teachers use them to support students' academic language or get writers started in a genre (e.g., Graff and Birkenstein 2014). We have adapted this idea to support students' reflective thinking about action, using particular words to move students forward toward positive action.

When we first ask students to complete the sentence stems, we print them off and hand them out. The specific phrasing depends on where we are relative to finishing one written piece and beginning another, but the emphasis is the same: What have you learned from your experience that you will carry forward? We use these stems, though you might adapt them for your own class:

- Because this time _____ ,

  next time I will _____ .

- Because last time _____ ,

  this time I will _____ .

The sentence stem strategy is quite simple, but the structured language yields some powerful, complex thinking. To help you understand the strategy in action, we use a recent experience with connective sentence stems as an example.

Model Sentence Stem Thinking

Our students had just finished writing informational books and had celebrated with a publishing party before school. Parents and other adults from around the school came for refreshments and the opportunity to read students' finished books (see also

Ayres [2013] for many ideas about ways to celebrate student work). It was a great before-school event, and students headed to their classrooms to begin the day buzzing with ideas about how it had gone as well as ideas for new pieces of writing.

Later in the morning, we gathered on the carpet for shared reflection. First, we simply asked for volunteers to share highlights from the party; then we segued into the sentence stem activity. We started by modeling the kinds of responses writers might make using the stems:

"Because this time I needed so many new terms while working on this book, next time I am going to try keeping a word list as I go."

"Because last time I ran out of time to do as much editing as I wanted to, next time I am going to reserve more time for editing."

"Because last time I used compare and contrast and it helped me generate some ideas for my writing, next time I am going to try it again and see if it helps."

With these examples, we were modeling both learning from a success and learning from a struggle or problem. Both are valuable, but we notice some students focus unhelpfully on one or the other. For example, some kids seem to name only that which they think they did poorly, vowing to do better next time. "Because I can't spell many words," they declare, "I will spell words better." This is a good start, as knowing what you need to work on is certainly part of improving. But ultimately, we think it's more productive to notice and reflect on how a writer *worked through* problems, not just identify them.

Similarly, nobody gets better from saying, "I'm good at this, so I did well at it." We want our students to plan for action over which they have agency, not simply perform to some fixed level of ability that is already there. We want them to focus on growth and the potential for change. Naming planned actions does this: it takes the emphasis off students' deficits and abilities and places it on how they deal with perceived deficits or how they can build on something they've done well. "You are the boss of your writing," we tell students. "You get to decide what to do as a writer, but then you need to *do* what you decide!"

The model reflections we offered also showed students that they could focus either on things they would do in the text (such as spell well, add details, include photos, or make a glossary) *or* on things they would do as part of a writing process (such as work with a partner, use time differently, or use an invention strategy). We find that our young writers sometimes gravitate toward product actions rather than process actions. Both are important, so we were careful to include both in our example sentences and also highlighted both when we responded to students' sentences.

Have Students Reflect and Complete the Stem

After we talked a bit about the examples we modeled, students took sentence strips of their own and moved off to complete at least one. Some grabbed more than one because, as we were talking, they thought of several future actions they wanted to take. Others students were more tentative, hesitant to name what went well this time that they would do again, so we talked with them a bit more until they felt ready to write. Often, for writers who are less confident, this sentence stem can be hard to complete. However, we see this as an opportunity, not a problem. Writers can plan action based on things they don't want to happen again just as much as they can on things that went well. We tell them, "No matter how hard or easy this writing was for you, there is something you can take from it into next time." We explain this to individual children, and we also make sure to get explicit about it in the whole-class sharing that follows.

Share Student Responses

As students finished their responses, we added each completed sentence to a chart; then we asked for volunteers to share. We knew their responses were likely to be as varied as the students themselves, and we knew they could learn so much from hearing how their peers reflected in this particular way.

Jia had been in the country for only a few months, and she was learning English. She composed her informational book in Chinese and then used Google Translate to provide a rough translation for members of the class. She looked forward to composing more and more in English, as she noted in this sentence she dictated in Chinese to a Chinese-speaking friend: "Because last time I can write down the sentences in English, next time I will write more." Jia was motivated to produce an intelligible English text, and she had a plan: to try to increase the number of sentences composed in English rather than rely only on Google Translate. (See Figure 4.1.)

Because last time I _can write down the sentences in English,_

next time I will _write more_ .

Figure 4.1 Jia's Completed Sentence Strip

Amelia, one of our most avid and fluent writers, noted how partner work had helped her and concluded from there that she would try using partners in a similar way next time. "Because last time I worked with others that were doing the same topic," she reflected, "next time I will work with others because that helps me." (See Figure 4.2.)

As part of our class, Amelia would always work with a partner, but we still saw her plan as significant because there would come a day when she'd no longer be in our class and following the procedures we were dictating. We're always mindful of this, and our greater goal is that students know what they can do independently to work through challenges in writing.

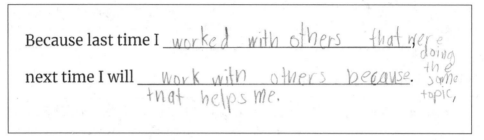

Figure 4.2   Amelia's Completed Sentence Strip

Students' plans for action also inform our teaching. Ryan noted something that helped with his organization and stated an intention to be more mindful of it when writing again: "Because last time I used it and it worked," he wrote, "next time I will use pros and cons." (See Figure 4.3.) During his informational writing about dogs, Ryan found pros and cons to be a successful way to organize his thoughts. We noticed that this gave us a chance to debrief what was successful about pros and cons while also highlighting other organizational strategies that Ryan could use to make his writing better.

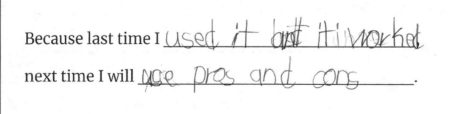

Figure 4.3   Ryan's Completed Sentence Strip

Meanwhile, Thomas identified a more motivational intention. He was a writer who tended to find other things to do around the classroom at the beginning of a writing period (for example, his pencils are very sharp!) or begin but then discard many pieces of writing. While we do want students to experiment with different writing ideas, at some point they also need to settle on something and draft it. Thomas knew this too, stating: "Because last time I played around with settings, next time I will JUST WRITE!" Noting that he was setting this intention for action helped us and his partners hold him more accountable for "just writing." (See Figure 4.4.)

Because last time I *played around with settings,*
next time I will JUST WRITE!

Figure 4.4   Thomas' Completed Sentence Strip

Darren's informational book was about Sonic the Hedgehog, a topic he knew a lot about. Darren sometimes struggled for ideas, that kind of kid you might see with his head down or not opening his notebook when writing time begins. When he did write, he sometimes needed one-on-one support to get from ideas to intelligible sentences. His book, completed with pride and with a lot of sweat and tears, was one of the highlights of our publishing party; it was by far the longest text Darren had ever written, and it had stretched his capacity for keeping up with papers over multiple days too. His informational text about Sonic, however challenging to complete, was a text he felt good about having written, and he carried this energy forward into plans to try a new kind of writing. Since he found in this piece that he "thinked a lot," he intended next time to try taking those thoughts into a new genre (one this class had not yet explored): "I will think about a poem." (See Figure 4.5.)

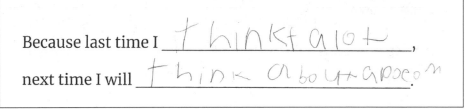

Because last time I think a lot,
next time I will think about a poem.

Figure 4.5   Darren's Completed Sentence Strip

Notice Common Themes

After everyone who wants to share has shared, we take time to point out what we've noticed. Our goal is to help students attend to the wide range of actions their writing experiences have suggested. Chief among our noticings is that some strips begin from something that went well, and other strips begin from a struggle. "I'm so glad we named both successes *and* struggles!" one of us remarks enthusiastically. "Both are so important to how we grow as writers. If we ignore the struggles, or hide them and try to pretend they didn't happen, then we'll never get better. Problems are so valuable!"

Overall, we see student writers using this strategy to both acknowledge a success or challenge in something they've just done *and* direct that knowledge toward future action. We think it is important for our students to understand that their writing doesn't just happen. What makes it more or less successful is not random. They *shape* their writing, and they can accumulate knowledge about how to shape it over time.

In a setting like ours, where a district-wide curriculum resource has us moving all students together through writing experiences in a sequence of genres, we especially value the way this strategy requires our students to look over the horizon from one genre to the next. In fact, in the examples we have just shown, our students didn't even know what unit was coming up next. They had to think instead about what learning could apply to whatever writing they might undertake in the future.

Figure 4.6 lists some other possible sentence stems you might try. These stems are less general and point writers in more specific directions.

Learning from a Problem and Solution	Because I solved the problem of _____ by _____, next time I will _____.
Building on an Experiment	Because last time I tried _____ and had the result of _____, this time I will _____.
Crossing Genres	Because in [genre] I _____, in [genre] I will _____.
Facing a Challenge	Because this time I struggled with _____, next time I will _____.

Figure 4.6   Ideas for Sentence Stems

invitation *to* REFLECT

These sentence stems also work for teachers. At the end of a unit, maybe even in the room while kids are doing their work with stems, try doing one of your own. Then (and this is important), record your action plans somewhere where you'll find them when planning next time:

- ◆ Maybe you'll tuck them into your plan book for next year. (We often start these early in the year before!)

- ◆ Or you might tuck them into the relevant pages of a unit resource you know you'll be using again next year.

- ◆ Or you could keep these plans in a Google doc and then set your phone to remind you around this time next year to look at your Google reflections from this year.

STICKY NOTE PLANNING

If you're like us, you sometimes are frustrated by the fact that you don't see students using the strategies you are teaching them enough in their own writing. You carve out time to have conversations about what writers do to revise their work to make it clearer for the reader. You unpack your thinking about how to improve writing as students share their work with the class or with partners. You spend time looking at mentor texts and noticing what authors do to make their writing engaging. You do all this teaching, and students seem to understand when they're with you in the minilesson, but when they go off to write, it seems the teaching doesn't follow them.

As we reflected on this problem in our own classroom, we knew that if our lessons were meant to help writers take action, we had to find a way to connect the teaching to the action more directly. The solution? For us, it all started with a simple pad of sticky notes. On these brightly colored little pieces of paper, we've taught our students to record plans for the actions they want to take. The notes are tangible markers, something different than the writing itself, so they stand out, and they always mean the same thing: *remember to do this*. We build shared understandings about their significance as we use the notes to record plans in different situations.

Imagine Planning Possibilities

If you've ever been in charge of planning activities for a vacation, you understand the importance of the "Don't Miss" or "Things to Do" section of your travel guide. Similarly, for students to become writers who plan their actions, they need to think specifically about "things to do" in writing. They learn about lots of things to do in minilessons, of course, but students also learn from the experience of writing. What's key is that students remember this learning and think of the options they have for action *before* we ask them to make plans. Here's an example of us moving from exploring options to sticky note planning.

One Tuesday morning, as we gather on the rug to wrap up our writing workshop session, Colleen asks students to think about what authors do when they revise. Sitting with their notebooks open in front of them, our students are silent at first, but then we see one hand go up and then a few more.

First the editing ideas surface, as they almost always do, even after many lessons about the differences between revision and editing. It's as if students need to clear the air with their editing concerns before they can even think about revision. We have learned that if we go ahead and hear a few of these editing intentions—many of them about spelling—then revision ideas will soon follow. For instance, Payton responds, "Writers check their spelling as they rewrite their stories."

Daniel, who is obsessed with writing in cursive (a new skill in third grade), says, "They do their best handwriting in their final copy."

"We are thinking as writers!" Colleen affirms, as she notes the editing concerns under a "Later" heading she's made on a chart. "But those can wait until later. For now, think about what you've been learning that you need to focus on. Think about how to make your stories *better*." We've been studying narrative, so the revision ideas are specific to stories.

Very quickly, new ideas pop up. Hannah, who is writing a story featuring her pet bearded dragon, Philip, says, "I need to work on making my beginning better so I can hook the audience."

"I need to reread my story to make sure it makes sense," shouts out Darren, who is totally invested in writing a story about two spiders who become fast friends.

Payton, who is writing a puppy pirate adventure on the high seas, says, "I still need to add more action by adding more details to my story." Soon, the children have generated a list full of actions they might take to revise their writing (see Figure 4.7).

Later	Now
Check spelling.	Choose a beginning.
Use best handwriting.	Add dialogue.
Rewrite [recopy].	Reread.
	Add action using five senses.
	Add more details.
	Describe setting.
	Reread to make sure it makes sense.
	Add cliff-hanger ending.

Figure 4.7   What Might We Do to Revise?

Decide on a Specific Action

Because Colleen has recorded their ideas on a chart, students now have clear, specific options in front of them. As Deana passes out the sticky notes, she asks each student to make a plan for tomorrow. "Write one thing from our list or write another that you think will be the best fit for moving your work forward. What do you need to do *specifically* to revise your story?"

As the students thoughtfully consider their work, they each make a commitment for the following day. Some glance up at the board and draw on the whole-group conversation; others keep their heads down and focus on their own drafts. Marcos writes, "Add a cliff-hanger ending," to wrap up his story about an adventure taking place at sea. Elsa writes that she wants to "add more dialogue" as she revises her story told from the perspective of our classroom pet, Chubbie. Each student makes a simple plan scrawled on a sticky note that he or she will carry out the next day. (See Figure 4.8 for kindergarten and 5th grade examples.)

The power in this process is in having students name *specific* actions they will take. If they are thinking only generally about working through a process like revision (or any other part of the writing process), then it's harder to be really intentional about their actions. A writer who is thinking, "Tomorrow I'm going to revise,"

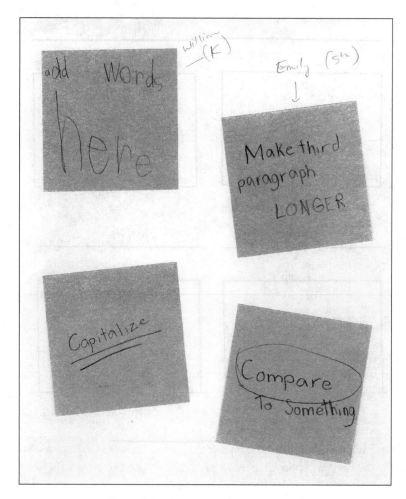

Figure 4.8   Sample Sticky Note Plans

is living toward that work very differently than a writer who is thinking, "Tomorrow I'm going to add a cliff-hanger ending." One has an idea about work; the other has a *plan*. And because the sticky notes are small, the actions have to be targeted.

Students place their sticky note plans on their writing at the point where they left off that day. The next day, they bring their notebooks and gather again on the carpet to start writing workshop. We remind them that they have left themselves notes. They find them easily, read over their plans, and quickly move off to work. The colorful notes capture the result of the whole reflective process: our students have *remembered* what they've learned, *described* that learning on their own terms, and then planned to take *action* to revise their writing. Each student has taken ownership and made his or her own plan. Not one of them says, "I have nothing to work on." They have all seen revision possibilities.

Across the year, our students see that we aim for growth more than mastery (Dweck 2006; Mraz and Hertz 2015) and that we appreciate where they are now and want them to have self-compassion toward their current struggles. We talk often about how writing, like any kind of learning, is a process—there's always more to do. The agency reflected in students' sticky note plans is key: they need to be able to plan *and act* for themselves. We know we shouldn't do it for them because we won't always be there to direct them, and this is why we put so much energy into teaching them how to plan their own future writing actions.

Plan with Partners

Because we use them so intentionally, sticky notes become a versatile tool students can use anytime they want to record a specific plan for action. Again, the presence of a note always means the same thing—*remember to do this*—so notes on drafts or in notebooks, placed at strategic points, serve as both visual and temporal reminders for writers.

We find that our students often reach for sticky notes when they work with partners to get ideas for revision. Through modeling, we teach students how to work together so that a partner gives the writer at least one specific idea for something to work on that will make the writing even better. The writer, of course, is responsible for deciding to take action (or not) on that advice, and the sticky note is a tool toward that end.

For example, during our informational writing unit, Ameena and Lin were sitting side by side, reading one draft at a time, chatting about the words and images on the page and asking questions. "I like your time line and your drawings of what animals lived during the Ice Age," Lin said.

As they read Lin's piece about plants out loud, Ameena shared an idea. "I feel like I am learning a lot about how plants grow. I wonder if you could add a life cycle picture to show how a seed grows into a plant." When partner time was up, both girls sat and thought for a moment before recording a plan for the next day's writing on a sticky note. Lin had taken Ameena's suggestions to heart and wrote that she would add pictures to show how a plant grows. (See Figure 4.9.)

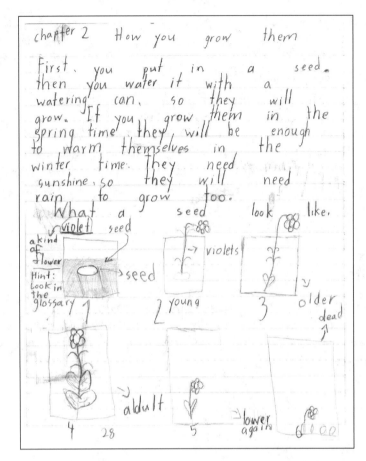

Figure 4.9   Lin's Plant Illustration

In many ways, partnerships provide another scaffold for the remembering and describing that lead to action. Often, children remember something they or the class learned earlier that makes sense for a partner now, and they present an option the writer might not otherwise have been able to consider. For example, Hannah and Tanya were both writing about animals for their informational books. After reading over one another's work, Tanya brought up the technical drawings of Madagascar hissing cockroaches we'd done in the fall in science, and she recommended that Hannah add a similar drawing of a bearded dragon. (See Figure 4.10.)

Figure 4.10   Hannah's Technical Drawing of a Bearded Dragon

All of this teaching—whole-group carpet conversations, charting, distinguishing between editing and revising, partner work—might seem like a lot just to get to one little plan made on a sticky note. In fact, when we started this practice, we used to just tell our students, "We're coming around with sticky notes. Write yourself a note about what you need to focus on tomorrow." That's how we would do it ourselves, as adults, right? But for our student writers, handing out notes and saying, "Make a note," wasn't enough. All of this scaffolded support is our way of showing students *how* a writer plans for action based on reflection. The process is complex and unfolds over time, as shown in Figure 4.11.

The process moves . . .

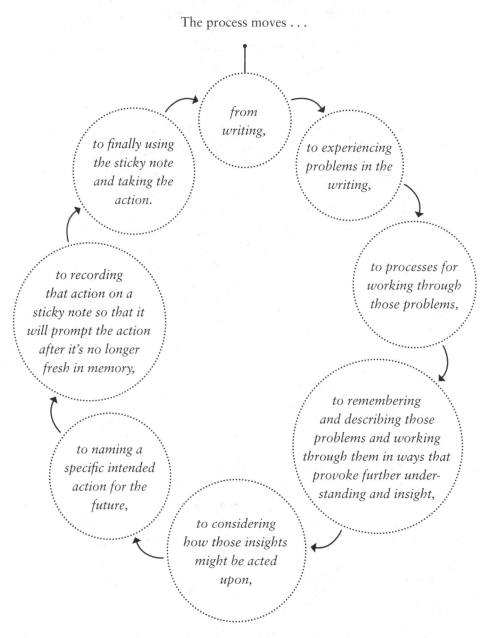

from
writing,

to experiencing
problems in the
writing,

to processes for
working through
those problems,

to remembering
and describing those
problems and working
through them in ways that
provoke further under-
standing and insight,

to considering
how those insights
might be acted
upon,

to naming a
specific intended
action for the
future,

to recording
that action on a
sticky note so that it
will prompt the action
after it's no longer
fresh in memory,

to finally using
the sticky note
and taking the
action.

And the whole cycle starts again.

Figure 4.11   Moving from Reflection to Action

To us, sticky note plans are more than simple reminders, like we might leave to remember to get milk at the store after work. They're more like cairns left as markers on a complicated woodland hiking trail.

ACCOUNTABILITY PARTNERS

Finally, we employ accountability partners to help students take action as writers. The idea is simple, and the focus is on ensuring that writers follow through on their plans. It's like when you set an intention to go to the gym more frequently. Having a partner can keep you accountable to that intention when you'd rather just sleep late. Your partner will be expecting you, and he'll know you didn't work out if you don't show up. It's not that the partner is really involved in your workout; it's that he gets you there and helps you follow through by simply being present. Our students sometimes use writing partners in a similar way, and interestingly enough, this strategy we now prescribe emerged organically and authentically in our students' work.

We first noticed students holding each other accountable in partnerships like the one between Thomas and Hunter. The boys paired up as they worked to revise their informational writing, and they both took the job very seriously. After sharing his piece about football, Hunter wrote himself a note to add a glossary to define some of the football terms used—a suggestion from Thomas. As they read over Thomas' piece about the ocean, Hunter recommended a Venn diagram to help compare and contrast features of the land with those of the water. Both boys recorded their plans on sticky notes, and the next day, when Hunter was finished adding his glossary, he rushed over to Thomas, notebook in hand, stating, "I just finished my glossary! Can you take a look at it?"

All on their own, Hunter and Thomas took the initiative to follow up and hold each other accountable. They understood someone was noticing their work in progress, and they became teachers for each other. The advice they shared enhanced their informational writing and left us free to confer with other students who needed support.

Like most writing teachers, we often have students work with partners during writing time, to collaborate or to provide feedback. Our students use partners to find out if their drafts make sense, to find passages where detail is needed, to compare strategies, and sometimes to help edit one another's work. However, having learned from watching students like Thomas and Hunter, we now also use partners very deliberately to support each other and hold each other accountable for taking action on reflection. We know the value of this strategy from our own experiences as teacher-writers. In books like *The Teacher-Writer* (Dawson 2016) and *Coaching Teacher-Writers* (Hicks et al. 2016), we've learned about writing groups where teachers sometimes meet to respond to each other's works in progress but just as often meet to set deadlines and share progress. This is metafeedback: feedback on writing processes and not just on the written text itself.

Partners Motivate

When students work together to hold each other accountable, they are almost always more motivated to engage deeply with process. Just like having a partner alongside you at the gym makes your workout less solitary, having a partner in the writing process makes the sometimes difficult work of writing less lonely. You try out something as you revise, and you have an audience who *cares* about what you're trying—and not just the impact on the writing but the fact that you tried at all. The message of accountability partnerships is "We're in this together!"

Figure 4.12   Partners Following Up on Each Other's Plans for Action

We saw how motivational having a partnership can be as we watched Adam and Jamal work together to revise their informational writing. Adam, who was writing about NFL football, and Jamal, who was writing about Minecraft, took their drafts and moved to the corner of the room by the door. As they shared, the laughter from the corner made Deana and Colleen a little nervous, but they tried to respect the partner time. As it turned out, the laughter indicated two writers who were completely engaged with each other's writing, and Jamal and Adam each walked away with specific plans for revision. Both boys, but Jamal especially, were motivated by their work together, and Jamal was determined to add the parts that would make his piece better, not just for himself but also for the partner who gave him the suggestions.

Partners Take Each Other Seriously

Having an accountability partner doesn't always mean taking that partner's suggestions; it simply means taking that person seriously and considering what she or he has to say. As students gain a stronger sense of themselves and their intentions as writers, they tend to cast a more critical eye on a partner's advice, a shift we celebrate.

Payton, for example, showed her own agency as a writer when she worked with Darren. Payton was writing about dogs, and Darren suggested she add a Venn diagram comparing cats and dogs. Payton was thoughtful about the suggestion, and she revisited her work with it in mind. She then explained, "The suggestion was a good one, but I already compared dogs with wolves, and I feel like that works better in my book." Payton realized the advice did not serve her author's purpose or direction, and more importantly, she realized she was in the driver's seat and could make her own decisions about what to include and what to omit.

Partners Become Independent

Once writers have the idea of using a partner for accountability (in addition to whatever content advice the partner may offer), they learn to do so more and more independently. And as using accountability partners becomes more routine, the roles partners play can also become a bit more specific. Over time, we teach students to advocate for themselves as writers by asking their accountability partners for specific kinds of help. Figure 4.13 lists some tasks for writers to consider assigning to a partner. You can also add to a list like this as you observe your students working in partnerships and ask them to reflect on the kinds of help they ask their partners to give.

- ◆ I plan to _____. Check with me on [date/time] to see whether I did this.

- ◆ I'm going off to write now. Can we meet at the end of writing time and check in?

- ◆ I'm sitting down next to you. Can you help me make sure to keep focused on my writing?

- ◆ I need to do some fast drafting. Time how long it takes me to write this [sentence/paragraph/page]!

- ◆ I'm noting on a sticky note that I will _____. Tomorrow, remind me this is here.

Figure 4.13   Possible Tasks for Accountability Partners

invitation *to* REFLECT

Writer Anne Lamott likes to say that the most powerful words in the English language are "me too." We know what she means. Teaching can be lonely, even discouraging, and even on the best days it is puzzling and hard work. Reflecting with a partner can help us think better and even feel better.

- Consider starting a breakfast club of teachers who meet before school to share experiences and questions.

- Get into a colleague's classroom, even if it's only for twenty minutes while your class is at PE. Have him or her do the same. What successes or concerns do you find you have in common?

- Join a community of teachers online. Ideas include the Teacher-Writer Network (on Facebook), Teachers Write (by subscribing to http://www.katemessner.com/blog), NCTE Connects (https://connects.ncte.org/), or the community of teachers who participate on the *Two Writing Teachers* blog (https://twowritingteachers.org/).

- Connect with colleagues in a professional association or network. Travel to an NCTE annual convention (see www2.ncte.org), your local NCTE state affiliate, or your local National Writing Project site (see www.nwp.org).

Overall, these strategies for planning and promoting action are merely prompts that help make it likely writers will do something with what they've learned through remembering and describing. Not every intended action will be carried out, we know (Does that happen in our own writing? In our own lives?), but we are signaling as strongly as we can that all of our work is always forward-looking; all learning experiences are cumulative. We're never doing something just that one time, even when the products we're making are never repeated. We're engaging in processes that over time will become familiar, as varied as they may be.

invitation *to* REFLECT

Anytime you write reflectively about an aspect of your teaching, these questions might help you turn toward action:

- ◆ What upcoming situation may be similar?
- ◆ What can I take forward from here?
- ◆ What specific action will I avoid in future?
- ◆ What specific action will I add?
- ◆ What possibilities remain?

chapter

FIVE

From Reflection to
Self-Assessment

Whether in our Tuesday sessions dedicated to reflection, in conferring with individual writers, or in quick minutes within minilessons or share time, we emphasize continual reflection. Remembering, describing, and acting on writing experiences are not about making separate moves one at a time. That is, we don't work on remembering in the first trimester, describing in the second, and acting in the third, and then consider that over the year we have taught reflection. No, reflection is a stance and activity that, at its best, includes all three components, working together simultaneously. And while we do teach each one directly, the parts themselves are not the end points; ultimately, we want students to develop deep and useful reflective practices that can help them—and us—to better know where they are in learning to write and where they might go next.

In this chapter, we step back and look more broadly at how all this reflection informs learning and teaching. We focus on reflection for student self-assessment across the linked moves of claiming an identity as a writer, setting goals, looking back at documents over time, communicating growth to parents, and learning from formal assessments.

Strategies for Self-Assessment

Kathleen Yancey (1998) writes: "If we don't ask our students to assess their own work—a process based on internal factors and criteria—they are likely to turn out . . . dependent on external rewards, not knowing where to begin to consider their own performances" (13). Maybe you, like us, recognize this problem from your own teaching: Children become overly focused on what started as a helpful system of rewards and consequences for behavior, and you realize the energy you're spending to maintain that system would be better spent on actually teaching. As you're introducing the next unit of study, someone asks, "Will we get a class party?" Or when you compliment a child for doing something kind, he asks, "Do I get a star ticket?"

As adults, nobody assesses us formally on how we are doing as parents, or as friends, or often even in our jobs—and when they do, the external rewards or consequences often don't feel all that meaningful. After all, when you put a lot of time and effort into cooking a great meal, and your kids just pick at it, does that mean you didn't do well? If you support a sick coworker by taking on some of her responsibilities, and nobody sees you do this or praises you for it, does that mean it wasn't a good thing to do? Of course not. You have ways of knowing how you are doing, and you have internal standards by which you can measure your efforts and your outcomes. Sometimes these are matched by external assessments—maybe you get a raise for high test scores—but more often, they're not; there's no value-added model for being an attentive listener to the children in your classroom, for instance.

We want student writers to have the power of self-assessment. The ability to know how they're doing and to make adjustments accordingly or to stay the course when things are working well is something writers can carry from class to class and well beyond the classroom, where stickers, pluses, grades, and other markers of progress or success cannot go. Self-assessment is also the most immediate form of differentiation for students with varied skill levels and needs: instead of reaching for a mark set by you and stopping there, students work toward their own standards, formed with clear knowledge about what they can do and what they are working toward. After all, in the world outside of school, no one will ever show up with a rubric for writing, but readers will understand or not, give writers the job or not, and be moved or not, and writers will feel pride, or make their point, or find that just-right word, or touch the heart they're after—or not.

CLAIMING AN IDENTITY AS A WRITER

We have said from the beginning that the development of writer identity is one of our goals in promoting reflection so intentionally. That is, we want children not only to write in class but also to *be* writers—writers who write inside and outside of school and who know what they can do and want to do as writers. When the going gets tough, these writers don't have to worry that they're somehow not smart or not capable—they can say to themselves, "OK. This is tough. But sometimes writing is tough! I am a writer, so I can draw on what I know about writing."

We pay explicit attention to writer identity from the very first days of writing workshop. As we described in Chapter 1, we use the stem, "I'm a writer who _____," to generate beginning, baseline statements about ourselves as writers that we compare with statements students make later as the year progresses. At the beginning of the year, many of our writers will complete the sentence, "I'm a writer who likes to write _____," with a favorite topic (dogs, Pokémon) or genre (stories, fantasy, comics). We value these statements and are happy to have writers who like to write at least some things!

The simplest version of the prompt simply lays down the sentence stem and then leaves space for students to complete it: "I'm a writer who _____." We encourage students to share and write wherever their thinking takes them. Some of our favorites include these statements:

- ◆ I am a writer who has struggled with racing, playing the piano, and writing when I can't concentrate.

- ◆ I am a writer who wants to write a twenty-page story.

- ◆ I am a writer who worries about her ideas if they are good or not.

- ◆ I am a writer who is proud of writing a lot.

- ◆ I am a writer who wants to try snowboarding down the driveway while eating a slushy and making a pea shooter.

At the beginning of the year, these statements give us insight into how students see themselves as writers, as well as how adept they are at self-evaluation. Some of the students can describe themselves in detail; others (and especially some of our younger students) struggle to consider what they're like as writers. Some describe their strengths proudly and readily; other kids (even accomplished writers) have trouble identifying any of their strengths.

We find that we are able to teach much more intentionally right from the start when we have clear, first-person portraits of each of our writers as they see themselves. And what's more, we think it's important to help students know *each other* as writers from the very start. So often, the getting-to-know-you activities teachers do at the beginning of the year establish common interests among students—these kids all like dogs; these three boys play soccer; this group of kids all moved over the summer— but we tend to do less to help kids get to know their classmates as learners.

As the year goes by, you can return to the prompt several times to help students consider their identities as writers and to gain insight into how their identities are growing and changing. Along with the general, open-ended stem, you might also expand the prompt to make it more specific. For example, you might add any of these:

◆ I'm a writer who has written _____.

◆ I'm a writer who likes to write _____.

◆ I'm a writer who worries about _____.

◆ I'm a writer who feels proud of _____.

◆ I'm a writer who has struggled with _____.

◆ I'm a writer who wants to try _____.

You should expect that over time, students' responses will become more reflective and rooted in the writing process. For example, later in the year one of our students responded, "I'm a writer who worries about if I have enough time and has struggled with finding a writing topic." Another wrote, "I'm a writer who has different ways of organizing my writing." Whether expressing a challenge or a strength, students learn to make statements about their capacities and concerns as they engage in writing processes.

You might find that some students need more support for completing the identity statements. At the beginning of the year, some students might not see themselves as writers at all. For them, completing this statement might be a bit like one of us completing a statement such as, "I am a leader who _____." "Am I a leader?" we may wonder. "What does this mean by 'leader,' and do the ways I lead count? Am I being immodest or too proud if I just jump in and say, 'Yes, I'm a leader'?" The statements are also challenging because they call for at least two layers of abstraction. First, students have to insert themselves into the frame "writer," and then they have to think within that frame. The child who writes, "I'm a writer who loves ice cream," needs support to see how to think within the specific frame of "writer."

One way to offer support is to tie the more general reflections to specific writing events. Who among us can easily say, "I'm a woman who . . . ," or "I'm a man who . . . ," and get specific? Yet we can speak with clarity about particular moments: "The day I hit the winning home run, I was a woman who felt the payoff of years of hard work and the sweetness of supporting teammates I loved, and who liked the feeling of winning so much, I was motivated to practice even harder!" It's the same with our student writers.

For example, in the middle of the year, our students wrote and published informational books on topics ranging from pets to video games to countries they'd visited. Following are a few of the responses they wrote specifically about this experience.

1. From writing this piece, I'm a writer who has learned _____.

   - writing can take a long time

   - lots from my partners

   - a lot about bearded dragons

   - my life is really interesting

   - writing can be fun but it is also hard

2. In this piece, I am a writer who has struggled with _____.

   - time

   - spelling

   - thinking of what to write

   - making it so you can understand my ideas

3. After this piece, I am a writer who feels proud of _____.

   - finishing this book

   - all of the work I finished

   - learning more English

   - getting a lot of information

   - my writing, of course!

We incorporated students' statements into "About the Author" pages, which they included at the end of their published informational books (see Figure 5.1).

In the last days of school, we gather our students together and consider the "I am a writer who _____" stem one last time. Sitting in a large circle, one of us typically begins: "I'm a writer who usually writes several drafts." The student next to

About the Author

I am the proud author of this book!

I am a writer who likes to write _about what I learn about._

From this piece, I am a writer who has learned _that writing can be fun but also hard_

In this piece, I am a writer who has struggled with _thinkin of ideas for this book_

I am a writer who feels proud of _all of the work I finished_

About the Author

I am the proud author of this book!

I am a writer who likes to write _about dogs, kids, holidays, and even monsters_

From this piece, I am a writer who has learned _that writing can take a long time_

In this piece, I am a writer who has struggled with _thinking about so much on the topic._

I am a writer who feels proud of _all the work I have done_

About the Author

I am the proud author of this book!

I am a writer who likes to write _about my life and other topic I'm intrested in_

From this piece, I am a writer who has learned _that my life is very intresting_

In this piece, I am a writer who has struggled with _some punctuation and spelling_

I am a writer who feels proud of _every book that I have made_

Figure 5.1   "About the Author" Pages

us follows, and then around the circle we go. We might make three or four rounds, as hearing others' ideas sparks kids' thinking. Some students will say, "Pass," after one or two rounds, and that's OK too.

"I'm a writer who has become better at coming up with ideas," says a writer who in September would wait for a teacher to come to his seat and prompt him before he felt he could begin writing.

"I'm a writer who used to write one page, but now I'm beginning to write a million pages," says one who in September would run up to a teacher, claiming, "I'm done!"

Pretty soon the stem itself falls away, and kids just describe who they're becoming as writers or what they see they've learned.

"I'm getting better at spelling, and I'm writing longer books," one child proclaims.

"I used to say, 'I can't do it,' but now I can do it," another says with a proud double thumbs-up.

"I keep trying."

"I'm writing stories that I like. That when I read over it, I enjoy it."

"I used to doubt myself a lot and say, 'No, this isn't good enough because hers is way better than mine.' But I think I've gotten better at trusting myself and self-motivation, telling myself I can do it."

These writers are all over the map in terms of their achievement in writing, but when asked what they're like as writers in June, they can comment on their strengths and weaknesses, on struggles and successes, on pieces they've written and habits they have acquired.

SETTING GOALS

We encourage students to use what they learn through reflection to set goals for themselves as writers across the year. On any given day, the goals different students are working toward are as varied as the students themselves. For example, here's a snapshot of some students' goals from one day in the fall:

- to spell better
- to write two or three pages in a day
- to use an idea from a book—like describing something how the author describes something
- to get better at handwriting
- to include more details [or more vivid details] in a narrative

- to avoid getting distracted by other people
- to use dialogue in a piece of writing
- to use different kinds of punctuation
- to try to write different types of narratives

We like students to have at least one active goal at all times. As they progress, one of us or the students themselves may decide that a goal has been met and it's time to set a new one, or we may revise the goal along the way.

Older students, of course, will likely have more sophisticated goals, as will any student later in the year. Fifth-grader Emily's current goal is to complete a submission for a local writing contest; kindergartner William's current goals include writing a book with chapters and learning how to use quotation marks. To us, what's most important is that students set goals for *themselves*, with a sense that reaching them is truly possible with some hard work during writing workshop.

invitation *to* REFLECT

What are your own goals? Take a few minutes to list some ideas. Any of these areas might be a space in which you want to articulate a goal:

- professional life
  - learning something new for your teaching
  - developing a new approach for some area
  - improving how you work with some specific population of students
- personal life
  - health
  - family
  - hobbies

As you work through the ideas in this chapter about goal setting with students, keep coming back to your own goals as well. What learning might be possible for *you* as a teacher with clear and consistent reflection?

In addition to the more general process and product goals students might have, we also have them set goals specifically connected to each unit of study. In our school, units of study for writing are organized around different genres. We don't, however, set goals at the beginning of a study, because students don't yet know enough about the genre they are learning to know what goals would make sense. Instead, we give students a little time to get a feel for the genre.

For example, in the first few days of a unit on opinion writing, our students read multiple opinion pieces, explore ideas that matter to them, and experiment with a few ways of framing opinion writing. They make starts at drafting, in an open-ended, experimental sort of way. In other words, lots of examples of opinion writing are in the air (and around the room), and students are close to choosing an idea to carry through a process toward publication. That's when it's time to set goals.

Imagine the Finish Line

A first step in goal setting within a unit of study is to establish a finish line for the writing. Students read multiple examples in the genre we're studying, so they know what finished writing looks and sounds like, but describing specific characteristics—which could become goals—can be a challenge. Students need language to frame their goals, and we have found that rubrics are helpful tools for this because they describe a standard for a piece of writing. We use rubrics, not to evaluate and score writing, but as a kind of menu from which students might select just one or two goals that *they* identify as important. The conversations we have around rubric descriptions help students envision what a final product might look like, but their goals are their own, situated within that vision.

Whether it's a district- or state-mandated rubric, or something from a resource we've been using, or even a rubric we've collaboratively constructed with our students as we looked at mentor texts, to move toward goal setting, we need a strong description of a finished product we can talk about. Most rubrics include broad categories students can use to think about their work—introductions, transitions, relevant details, elaboration, spelling, punctuation, and so on.

Typically, we have students work with rubrics in small groups. We ask them to think about the writing they've done so far and consider it in light of the finish line captured in the rubric. The students sit together, looking between the writing in their notebooks and the rubric. We ask them to share evidence from their notebooks with their group mates before marking "Not Yet," "Starting To," or "Yes" for each indicator, such as "I introduced my piece in a way that grabs the reader's attention."

We remind them that these are just drafts, even snippets of drafts, that they're looking at so far, so of course most items will be in the "Not Yet" category. That's appropriate for works in progress, after all.

Finally, we ask students to look over the "Not Yet" column and think about which indicator would be most beneficial to their writing. By the end of writing workshop that day, students set one personal goal for the unit.

Like us, you may need to make adjustments in this process for the many writers in your class. For example, we are careful to group students with similar needs together, and we strategically place adults with groups that might need more support. Sometimes, we use different rubrics with different small groups as their needs indicate. For example, our ESL friends have picture supports accompanying their rubrics. Some groups might do better with the rubric from a grade below or a grade or two above.

The point is, we make every effort to set students up for success with a checklist that connects to their abilities. Students—like everyone else learning something new—are more motivated and interested when their goals are realistic and attainable. We want to lift up our writers, so it's important to us to have a checklist in front of every writer on which he or she can check "Yes" at least once or twice. For some kids, a conventions focus might be using initial capitals and final periods; for others, attention to paragraphing is more appropriate. Students should be moving toward a finish line that they both *want* to reach and *have a chance of* reaching.

Make an Action Plan

Goals are important, but we want students to turn their goals into *action plans* that will move them toward those goals. After all, you might set a goal for yourself to run a marathon, but saying that alone won't get you across the finish line. You'll need a plan for specific actions that will help you get closer to the goal—taking carefully sequenced intermediate distance runs, for instance, or adopting a new regimen of weight training. The same goes for student writers: they need to identify specific actions that will move them toward their goals.

To help students make concrete action plans for their goals, we prompt them to think about two questions:

1. What helps with the goal?
2. What gets in the way?

Then we show students how to reframe their responses as actions. For example, if a student has a goal to write longer pieces, and he says what helps him write longer is having a quiet spot to work in, then "Find a quiet spot to work in" becomes part of his action plan. If he says what gets in the way is that sometimes he runs out of ideas, we might say, "Hmm, OK, sounds like you need to spend some more time prewriting before jumping into writing a draft." We have him list a few prewriting strategies he's learned that he'll commit to trying before he starts drafting.

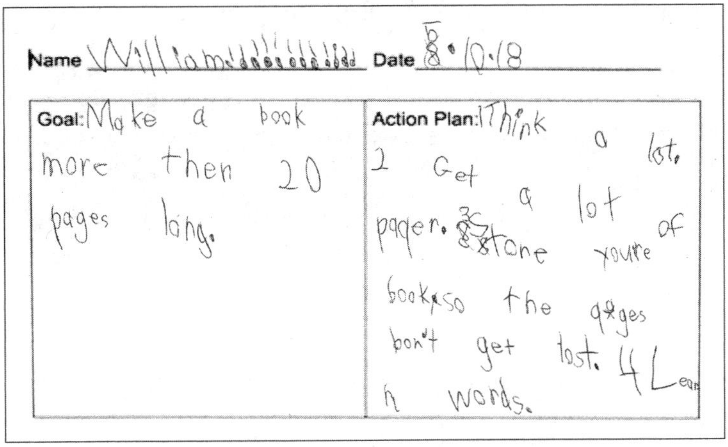

Name William	Date 8·10·18
Goal: Make a book more then 20 pages long.	Action Plan: Think a lot, 1 Get a lot of paper. 3 Store youre book so the pages don't get lost. 4 Learn words.

Figure 5.2 William's (Grade K) Action Plan

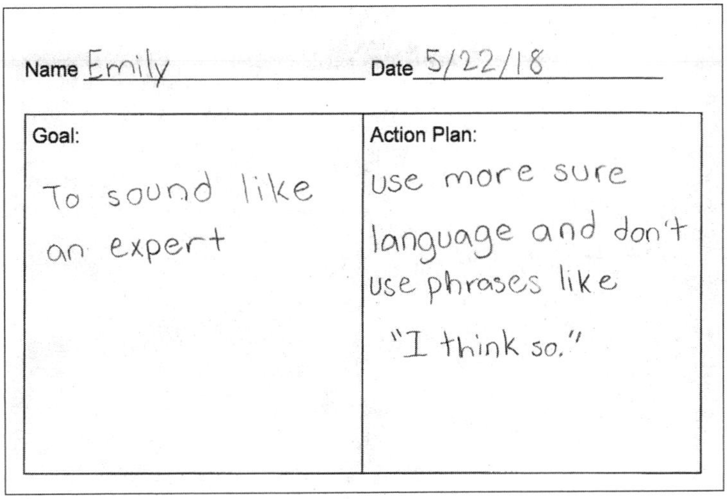

Name Emily	Date 5/22/18
Goal: To sound like an expert	Action Plan: use more sure language and don't use phrases like "I think so."

Figure 5.3 Emily's (Grade 5) Action Plan

We often use our own writing to model moving from a goal to an action plan and we invite students to help us think of possibilities. Doing this as a whole class first supports students when they move to construct their individual action plans. In our opinion unit, for example, students planned to take action to address a range of writing goals they set for themselves:

- Jamal, who was writing to his dad about playing a new video game together, felt his letter was more fact than opinion, so he simply stated that he needed to focus on his audience and make sure it sounded like an opinion piece.
- Thomas, who was writing to his family members about the problems regarding texting while driving, wanted to revisit his beginning. He decided to develop three different beginnings and choose the best one.
- Jason decided he needed to organize his writing in order for it to make sense, so his plan was to grab some loose leaf paper and rewrite it.
- Euna felt like she had worked hard and could check off all the boxes in the rubric, but she still created an action plan for adding more evidence, because she felt it would make her writing even stronger.

Each child walks away from this activity with a plan in place that he or she can act upon immediately during our writing time. It isn't just "I need to work on this," but "I need to work on this, and *this* is how I am going to do it."

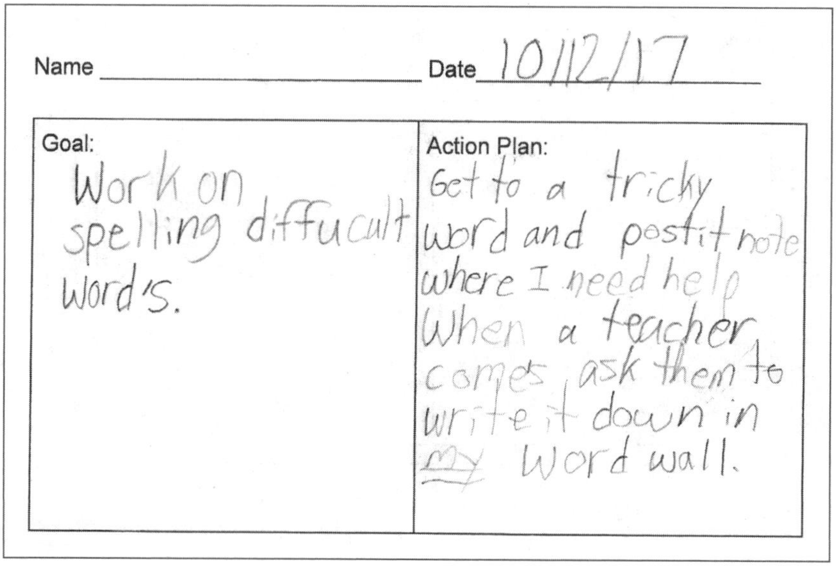
Name ____________ Date 10/12/17

Goal:	Action Plan:
Work on spelling diffucult word's.	Get to a tricky word and postit note where I need help When a teacher comes ask them to write it down in my word wall.

Figure 5.4 Another Sample Action Plan

REFLECTING THROUGH DOCUMENTS: THAT WAS THEN; THIS IS NOW

To help students notice their growth in specific aspects of writing over time, we have them compare artifacts they've created across the year. For example, we might have students reflect on the following:

- the entire corpus of notes, drafts, and finished work for two different finished pieces of writing

- artifacts of a given strategy used multiple times over the year, such as outlines or organizers for all their different pieces of writing

- parallel passages from different texts, such as just the leads from all of their different pieces of writing

One Thursday morning midyear, for example, we had students work in small groups as they studied two of their notebooks, one from the beginning of the year with narrative writing and the second with informational writing. We asked them to use sticky notes to notice the similarities (pink notes) and differences (green notes) between the two notebooks, and we encouraged them to talk about what they were finding.

After the small groups worked for ten or fifteen minutes or so, we came together to talk about what they noticed. We heard several students murmur in agreement as they heard peers say things that resonated with their own experience, and we saw some make a silent "oh yeah" hand gesture of agreement in their laps. We saw eyebrows go up and then smiles spread across faces as classmates reported something that at first seemed strange but then started to make sense. Figure 5.5 lists some of the similarities and differences the students noticed when they compared their notebooks.

Same	Different
topics and interests	length of writing
pictures in both	talking marks
circled words	more detailed work—illustrations and text
crossed-out words	second book was less sloppy
brainstorming ideas (heart map, expert list)	added more text features
similar writing style (numbering sentences)	real things versus fictional things
hard work	"My spelling got better. I used to spell *they* like *thay* and now I spell it correctly."
wrote about real stuff	
wrote about not-real things, but one was telling people about it	

Figure 5.5 Similarities and Differences Students Noted

The value in comparing writing done in different genres, as we did here, is that students have an opportunity to see how various writing strategies do and don't apply equally in different writing situations across genres. Editing strategies, for example, are going to prove fairly consistently useful, with exceptions for genre-specific features of a text, such as dialogue in a narrative or citations in a presentation of research. But strategies for invention might not vary much at all: partner brainstorming, drawing a picture, and quickwriting can be helpful in most writing situations. When students come to realize this from looking at their own work, they are more likely to include more nimble strategies in a repertoire of options that, over time, they choose to use without any prompting from us.

As students compare documents, you might prompt them with questions like these (adapt the language to your students' age and experience):

- When comparing texts students have written in different genres, you might ask them about what similarities and differences they notice in

  - how the texts are organized and the parts they include
  - the voice or word choices they made in each text
  - the conventions that were important to use in each text
  - where they had difficulty and where they felt the writing was easy
  - the amount or kind of revision they had to make in each text

- When comparing initial and subsequent texts students have written in the *same* genre, you might ask:

  - "What similarities do you see in the structure of these two texts? In the themes or ideas? In conventions?"
  - "What differences do you see? *Why* are they different?"
  - "Are there strategies that worked especially well for you as you developed each piece in the genre?"
  - "What are your strengths in writing in this genre?"
  - "How do you want to grow as a writer in this genre?"

- When comparing multiple iterations of the same strategy (e.g., prewriting for different pieces of writing; developing multiple leads for different pieces of writing), you could ask:

  - "What circumstances led you to use that strategy in each situation? What did those situations have in common?"

♦ "Did the strategy have the same effect each time? Different effects? If different, how do you account for those differences?"

The specific questions you ask matter less than the deliberate practice of noticing a difference and then reflecting to account for the difference. By comparing past and present documents, be they notebooks, finished products, or something else, students have the opportunity to notice and name their growth as writers. They don't have to wait for a teacher's assessment to know that they have improved; they can see for themselves the difference their hard work has made. With document reflection, students also have the opportunity to notice what stays consistent over time—both the strategies they go back to again and again that they can claim as their own and the struggles they face and want to address as they move forward.

COMMUNICATING GROWTH TO PARENTS

In both fall and spring, our district sets aside two days for students to come to school with their parents for conferences, almost always with the students present during the meeting. Students are active in the conference, collaborating with both their parents and the teacher to share how they are moving toward goals and identifying needs. For the writing portion of the parent conference, our students use reflection before the conference to prepare to share their writing goals with parents.

In a classroom where reflection and self-assessment are intentional and frequent, the work of setting goals is already done—students simply talk about whatever their current finish-line goals and action plans are when conference time approaches. They can note their goals on a written conference plan, display them on a Google slide to show parents at the meeting, or write them on the outside of a folder of writing they will be sharing. Then, they assemble examples of their work that show parents how they are working to address their needs and meet their goals.

At the conference, kids take the lead, sharing goals and achievements and showing evidence from their work. Because we reflect and talk about our work so often, students are comfortable in this role, and it shows. They sit up a little straighter, they speak with clarity and confidence, and their parents sit on the edge of their seats as children read passages from their work, such as "My Trip to the Beach" or "Adopting Maddie." Parents, who might otherwise focus on errors in conventions if we just handed them samples of student writing, are simply mesmerized when they sense the ownership and self-direction their children display when discussing their own goals and progress as writers. Even our most struggling writers can talk about what they are working on and what it might take to get there; instead of focusing on deficits only, we focus on growth.

In spring conferences, we have students review and compare writing samples from across the year, sharing with parents the same "noticings" they discovered for themselves when they compared various writing documents and reflected on what they noticed (described earlier).

Here are some ideas for how you might have your students prepare for three-way conferences where they will share their work with their parents and you:

- Students can create a brief slideshow using a basic three-slide format: (1) a writing goal, (2) evidence from their work that shows the need for the goal, and (3) action plans to meet the goal. These can focus on goals in progress, or they can celebrate goals the students have accomplished already. At the conference, students can present the slides with narrative commentary.

- Students can create a storyboard or comic narrating their growth as a writer along some dimension, with panels depicting (1) the goal they set, (2) the action steps they took toward that goal, and (3) how they knew they had achieved the goal. At the conference, these might be displayed in the hall for parents to view, or students might include them in a portfolio of items across subject areas.

- Students can select a piece of their writing that they feel shows their best work to date and upload a photo of that work to Seesaw or any other online sharing platform. They can then add audio commentary to describe how they worked through goal setting and action plans to reach that point. Either you can share these with parents electronically before a conference and then discuss them at the meeting, or students can display the photos and play the commentary for parents to hear at the meeting.

Many students who have encountered academic difficulty *or* those who have had problems with classroom behavior dread conferences. If your parents and your teacher always seemed to focus on your problems or struggles, wouldn't you feel the same way? But when student writers take the lead in their own conferences and share their self-assessment, both positive and negative, there's more room for an actual conversation. We still can talk frankly about places where growth is needed, but it happens in terms the students name for themselves and that always are contextualized in possibility.

LEARNING FROM FORMAL ASSESSMENTS

Like many others, our district mandates a formal, timed, on-demand writing assessment following the completion of a unit of study, and our state has required a similar assessment at the end of the year in grades 3–8. Many students give these assessments their best shot, but we also have had students tear papers, cry, refuse to write, and have all other manner of reactions. Robbie, for example, sat staring at a blank page when we gave the assessment on narrative writing with the prompt "Write about one time in your life, a small moment." It seemed quite open-ended, but when Deana approached him to encourage him to get his ideas down, he looked up and said, "You know me, Mrs. Washell. I cannot think about what to write. I need more choice than this." Robbie had wowed us with his narrative writing more than once, but especially with his "Magic Pencil" story that was filled with descriptive language, meaningful dialogue, and an engaging lead. Now, as he sat staring at his blank test paper, it was clear that this assessment would not adequately paint a picture of the writer Robbie truly was.

When you have a writing workshop in which students have some agency over the pacing and progress of their work, and then an outside assessment contrasts with that, students will push back, at least internally if not out loud. The answer cannot be to ignore their observations or frustration. After all, we spend the year helping students get better at noticing their own needs as writers through reflection; we don't want to stop doing so suddenly when it's testing time. Instead, we've learned to invite students into a reflective conversation and help them process the differences between the writing they normally do in writing workshop and the writing they do on more formal assessments. These reflective conversations support students' agency as writers and also help them think strategically about writing for tests.

One year, for example, our students were shocked when we gave them a required test prompt that asked them to complete—in two class periods—an informative piece of writing that would teach an audience about something. Quickly, hands shot up to protest the time restraint. In the unit preceding the assessment, our students had worked for weeks to thoroughly develop an informational book, and now they had only two days? They knew themselves as writers, and they knew that to do their best work, it would take time to think, write, reflect, write some more, revise, write even more, and then edit. With some coaxing, our students wrote something, but we knew that something didn't always reflect who they truly were as writers.

The day after the informational writing assessment ended, Deana and Colleen invited the children to reflect on the experience. "Let's compare and contrast the writing you did this week on the assessment and the writing you did over the unit. How are they the same and how are they different?"

At first, the students were mostly quiet, with one or two kids popping their hands up to share ideas about what was the same. With more time, they began to add more, piggybacking off one another's thinking, and we recorded their ideas in a Venn diagram (see Figure 5.6).

The class agreed that both pieces of writing served the same purpose—informing others—but students also pointed out many differences. "When I wrote my informational book about dogs," Payton shared, "my audience was anyone who was interested in learning more about dogs along with my parents, but in the assessment, only the teachers are the audience for my writing."

"I also learned a lot from working with a partner when I wrote, but this time I had to work quietly all by myself," Elsa commented.

As we reflected together, our students considered purpose, audience, and process across two different writing situations, and while many of their reflections were about the limitations they perceived, sometimes students felt their experiences in units helped them perform better on formal assessments. Amelia, for example, shared, "Because we learned so much about informational writing when we did our own, I feel like this writing [assessment] was much easier because I knew exactly what to do."

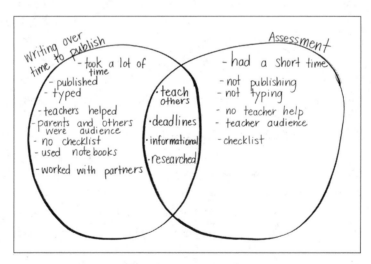

Figure 5.6   Venn Diagram Comparing Workshop Writing with
Timed Assessment Writing

So much of our reflection all year long is about noticing and responding to conditions. What am I experiencing as a writer? Why did this happen? What can I learn from it? What control might I take over this situation? What choices are available to me now? These are the kinds of questions that reflective writers can ask and answer. When we help students view a formal writing assessment through reflective eyes, we help them to take charge of the high-stakes situations in which they are being evaluated.

This type of reflection is valuable for older students as well. Anne and two of her colleagues worked together to help middle and high school students reflect across writing experiences in three genres: a whole-class genre study of nature writing, an independent genre of each student's choosing, and a whole-class study of writing for standardized tests (Whitney, Ridgeman, and Masquelier 2011). So much came out of these reflections. For example, the students were surprised to learn that readers of the state tests had less than three minutes to read each essay! They quickly concluded that they would need to state their main idea much earlier in their essays—and much more explicitly—than usual. When writers reflect on differences between writing for assessment and other writing situations they experience, they can be more strategic about how to respond to the demands of different writing tasks.

The nature and number of formal assessments teachers administer varies by locale and the policies and pressures in a particular context. But whatever formal assessments are in place, what matters most is that we know as much as we can about what students are thinking about as they write. To help them develop, we need intimate insight into what motivates students' decisions. We need to know what they notice about their own practice and where they might have blind spots. We need to understand how their feelings are interacting with the content we teach—where they are taking bold steps as writers and where they are afraid to try. We need to know what their priorities are and how these coincide or differ from our own.

By listening carefully to students' reflections, we come to understand much more deeply the impact of our teaching, because we get to see not only what students do in response to instruction but also how they take it up—what they make their own, what they change. Reflection is an "assets-forward" information source that stands in contrast to assessments designed only to highlight deficits. We value both kinds of information, but through reflection we frame our students' work positively and with deep appreciation for the very hard work they do as writers—regardless of their objective level of accomplishment at any given moment.

invitation *to* REFLECT

Teachers, too, experience outside assessments, such as programs of teacher evaluation, teacher report cards developed by a district or state, or local shared self-assessment activities. Sometimes these provide useful information and feel like purposeful, integrated parts of our work; other times they are imposed from outside, for purposes defined by others, and feel like impositions or even insults. Try reflecting on some of these assessments using the strategies we have described here.

- What can you learn about how you might approach such assessments in the future?
- What can you learn about how you might respond to the results of such assessments?

Where Reflection Takes Us

In the first pages of this book, we laid out a vision: writers who know for themselves what they are doing and why. We want a classroom in which students are the ones doing most of the work, engaging with writing because there are things they wish to say, and working toward saying them using knowledge about writing that they build from experience, not just from being told. This is the vision we take with us into the classroom and that we have tried to share with you here.

We're a lot like the writers we teach every day: we may not reach every goal, every time, but we do see our own improvement, because we deliberately return to reflect on what we are learning day by day. Just like our student writers, we have tools for remembering what we've experienced in the classroom so far, for describing what we're noticing over time, and for making action plans that move our practice forward. Just like a student's draft, our work is a work in progress. We look forward to where reflection will take us next.

Works Cited

Ayres, Ruth. 2013. *Celebrating Writers: From Possibilities Through Publication*. With Christi Overman. Portland, ME: Stenhouse.

Boud, David, Rosemary Keogh, and David Walker. 1985. *Reflection: Turning Experience into Learning*. London: Routledge.

Brown, Peter C., Henry L. Roediger III, and Mark A. McDaniel. 2014. *Make It Stick: The Science of Successful Learning*. Cambridge, MA: Belknap/Harvard UP.

Calkins, Lucy McCormick. 1994. *The Art of Teaching Writing*. New ed. Portsmouth, NH: Heinemann.

Damico, Nicole, and Anne Elrod Whitney. 2017. "Turning Off Autopilot: Mindful Writing for Teachers." *Voices from the Middle* 25 (2): 37–40.

Dawson, Christine M. 2016. *The Teacher-Writer: Creating Writing Groups for Personal and Professional Growth*. New York: Teachers College Press.

Dewey, John. 1933. *How We Think*. Lexington, MA: Heath.

Dweck, Carol. 2006. *Mindset: The New Psychology of Success*. Vol. 19. New York: Random House.

Graff, Gerald, and Cathy Birkenstein. 2014. *They Say/I Say: The Moves That Matter in Academic Writing*. 3rd ed. New York: W. W. Norton.

Hicks, Troy, Anne Elrod Whitney, James Fredricksen, and Leah Zuidema. 2016. *Coaching Teacher-Writers: Practical Steps to Nurture Professional Writing*. New York: Teachers College Press.

Johnston, Peter H. 2004. *Choice Words: How Our Language Affects Children's Learning*. Portland, ME: Stenhouse.

Mraz, Kristine, and Christine Hertz. 2015. *A Mindset for Learning: Teaching the Traits of Joyful, Independent Growth*. Portsmouth, NH: Heinemann.

Schön, Donald A. 1991. *The Reflective Practitioner: How Professionals Think in Action*. London: Routledge.

———. 1995. "The New Scholarship Requires a New Epistemology." *Change: The Magazine of Higher Learning* 27 (6): 27–34.

Goal: build strong identities as writers
(not produce good writing or get better at writing)

Smith, Frank. 1988. *Joining the Literacy Club: Further Essays into Education.* Portsmouth, NH: Heinemann.

Stafford, Kim. 1996. "Quilting Your Little Solitudes: How to Write When You Don't Have Time To." *Teachers and Writers* 27 (5): 4–8.

Taylor, Rebecca D., Eva Oberle, Joseph A. Durlak, and Roger P. Weissberg. 2017. "Promoting Positive Youth Development Through School-Based Social and Emotional Learning Interventions: A Meta-Analysis of Follow-Up Effects." *Child Development* 88 (4): 1156–71.

Whitney, Anne Elrod, Michael Ridgeman, and Gary Masquelier. 2011. "Beyond 'Is This OK?': High School Writers Building Understandings of Genre." *Journal of Adolescent and Adult Literacy* 54 (7): 525–33.

Yancey, Kathleen Blake. 1998. *Reflection in the Writing Classroom.* Logan: Utah State University Press.

Remember

The first step to reflecting is remembering
which we might sometimes take for granted
How did you know this had to be supported?
How do you support young writers to remember?
"I am a writer who..."
Remember — what / how / why
declarative / procedural / contextual / conditional
presumes intention

→ Remembering strategies
"meaningful arc of connected experiences / activities" not "one damned thing after another"
"Notebook as an important record of practice"

Photo elicitation